D0911189

PENGUIN CANADA

JUSTIN BIEBER

CHAS NEWKEY-BURDEN is the author of a number of acclaimed biographies of such subjects as Simon Cowell, Michael Jackson, Amy Winehouse, Alexandra Burke and Paris Hilton. His work has been translated into nine languages. He is co-author, with Julie Burchill, of *Not in My Name: A Compendium of Modern Hypocrisy.*

JUSTIN BIEBER

The Unauthorized Biography

CHAS NEWKEY-BURDEN

PUFFIN
CANADA

PUFFIN CANADA

Published by the Penguin Group

Penguin Group (Canada), 90 Eglinton Avenue East, Suite 700, Toronto, Ontario, Canada M4P 2Y3
(a division of Pearson Canada Inc.)

Penguin Group (USA) Inc., 375 Hudson Street, New York, New York 10014, U.S.A.
Penguin Books Ltd, 80 Strand, London WC2R 0RL, England
Penguin Ireland, 25 St Stephen's Green, Dublin 2, Ireland (a division of Penguin Books Ltd)
Penguin Group (Australia), 250 Camberwell Road, Camberwell, Victoria 3124, Australia
(a division of Pearson Australia Group Pty Ltd)
Penguin Books India Pvt Ltd, 11 Community Centre, Panchsheel Park, New Delhi – 110 017, India
Penguin Group (NZ), 67 Apollo Drive, Rosedale, North Shore 0745, Auckland, New Zealand
(a division of Pearson New Zealand Ltd)
Penguin Books (South Africa) (Pty) Ltd, 24 Sturdee Avenue, Rosebank, Johannesburg 2196,
South Africa

Penguin Books Ltd, Registered Offices: 80 Strand, London WC2R 0RL, England

Published in Canada by Penguin Group (Canada), a division of Pearson Canada, Inc., 2010.
Simultaneously published in Great Britain by Michael O'Mara Books Limited, 9 Lion Yard,
Tremadoc Road, London SW4 7NQ.

1 2 3 4 5 6 7 8 9 10

Copyright © Michael O'Mara Books Limited, 2010

Manufactured in Canada

Library and Archives Canada Cataloguing in Publication data available upon request to publisher
British Library Cataloguing in Publication data available

ISBN 978-0-14-317837-8

Visit the Penguin Group (Canada) website at **www.penguin.ca**

Special and corporate bulk purchase rates available; please see **www.penguin.ca/corporatesales**
or call 1-800-810-3104, ext. 2477 or 2474

Contents

Justin Bieber in numbers

0.27   the percentage of all Tweets written that have mentioned Justin

2   the minutes it reportedly takes Justin to solve a Rubik's Cube

3   the minutes it once took Justin to sign fifty posters

5   the minutes it takes Justin to style his hair in the morning

6   Justin's favourite number

10   the countries in which *My World* was a Top 30 hit

12   the age Justin was when he competed in the Stratford Star competition

13   the age Justin started dating

2007   the year in which Justin opened his YouTube account

3,755   how many Tweets Justin had written as of June 2010

30,461   the estimated population of Stratford, where Justin grew up

1.5 million   the number of Tweets written about Justin's debut album (as of June 2010)

18.1 million   the number of Tweets that mentioned 'Justin Bieber' in the same period

23.7 million   the number of Tweets that mentioned 'Bieber' in the first six months of 2010

Introduction

n April 2010 Justin Bieber performed live in front of 30,000 adoring spectators in Washington DC, the capital city of America. For a sixteen-year-old boy this is a pretty remarkable feat in itself – but it gets even more amazing than that. The performance took place at the White House, and among the 30,000 people in the audience was the couple who live there – the President of the United States of America, Barack Obama, and his wife Michelle. The First Lady was spotted dancing along to Justin's songs. Incredible, and all the more so given that this was the second time young Justin had sung for her and the President! The venue for this performance – the powerbase of a global superpower – was appropriate because Justin himself has become nothing short of a superpower of the pop world over the past few years.

He now has millions of fans across the globe, but to describe his devotees as 'fans' is an understatement: their devotion to Justin goes far beyond normal fandom. The crazy whirlwind of excitement that follows him wherever he goes is known as 'Biebermania'. He has experienced it across the globe, from a fans' stampede in Australia to similar scenes of hysteria in New Zealand, Paris and New York – and everywhere in between.

As he flies in to any country, huge crowds flock to the airport to greet him. The countries might be different but the scenes are always the same: thousands of admirers crying, screaming and jostling to get closer to him. These hyperventilating fans have also created their own language in which to express their devotion: 'OMB' means 'Oh My Bieber'; a 'Belieber' is one who 'believes in Justin'; a 'Bieberholic' is, as Justin himself put it, someone 'who is addicted to the Bieb'.

As his fame and popularity soar, Justin must sometimes look back to how it all began: with a humble account on the YouTube website onto which he and his mother uploaded videos of him singing. They originally only expected these clips to be watched by relatives and a few friends. But the moment they clicked the 'upload' button on the first video – on 19 January 2007 – they set in motion a chain of events that would quickly make Justin one of the most famous people on the planet.

Fate would lift him and his mother from their humble existence in a small town in Canada to the very heart of the music industry in America. There, the record company boss who gleefully signed him believed he had found a star who could be as successful as The Beatles, Elvis Presley and Michael Jackson rolled into one.

Justin has never forgotten where he came from – and

neither should we. It is tempting for the public to look at him now and think he is a very lucky boy. His lifestyle is certainly to be envied, but before fate dealt Justin the lucky hands of fame, fortune and success, it had already set him some tough, even heartbreaking, obstacles to overcome. His incredible life story has been a rollercoaster, from the highest of highs to the lowest of lows and back again. It really is like something from the movie world, a blockbuster film with a fascinating plot full of drama and inspiration.

Let's start at the beginning . . .

1

A Star is Born

ustin Drew Bieber was born at 12.56 a.m. on 1 March 1994 in a city in Canada called London. He grew up in a small city called Stratford, which lies in the Canadian province of Ontario. He has described his home city as 'a little town of 30,000 in the middle of nowhere', and he has also said that 'nothing ever came out of Stratford'. Justin's millions of fans around the world would disagree – and so might some Stratford residents. Those who have studied their Canadian history would point out that, as well as Justin, other famous people *have* lived in Stratford, including Thomas Edison – the man who invented the light bulb. But for millions of girls around the world, the only person to have come out of the town who really matters is Justin Drew Bieber.

So what is the area Justin grew up in really like? Stratford is a charming and mostly tranquil place, which was voted 'the prettiest city in the world' in 1997, when Justin was merely a three-year-old toddler. It is named after the English market town of Stratford-upon-Avon, an area most famous for being the birthplace and childhood home of the celebrated playwright William Shakespeare. The Canadian Stratford is rightly proud of the connection and it hosts an annual Shakespearean Festival across its theatres, outside one of which Justin busked as a child.

Just as the town he was born in is named after the capital city of England, some of Stratford's roads and rivers are named after English places. Like most residents, Justin was charmed by the swans – both white and black – which glide gracefully along the River Avon (which, in keeping with the English theme, was originally called the Thames). Near the river is an impressive park that also held plenty of wonder for him as he grew up.

Justin's parents, Jeremy and Pattie, were overjoyed by the birth of their child, a small but very healthy baby. They positively doted on him from the start and were naturally hugely proud of him. As most new parents do, they discussed which of them he most resembled. The truth was that he had inherited a mixture of their respective features: his eyes and nose resembled those of his father, but his lips were pretty much the same as his mother's. Justin's birth brought light and happiness into their lives.

However, the sad reality is that their marriage began to unravel in the years after Justin's birth. Eventually, Jeremy and Pattie separated and divorced. Jeremy moved to Winnipeg in the Canadian province of Manitoba. Pattie, who was awarded full custody of their son, remained in Stratford where she herself had grown up. She changed her surname back to her maiden name and from then on was known as Pattie Mallette, though she agreed that Justin should keep his father's surname of Bieber.

The family had never been especially wealthy, and once she became a single mother Pattie faced quite a struggle to keep them afloat. Consequently, Justin grew up in humble public housing in one of the poorer neighbourhoods of Stratford. Times could be tough, but he was a sweet child and, whatever financial challenges his mother faced, Justin was never short of love thanks to her devotion.

Looking back during an interview with the Canadian weekly magazine *Maclean's*, Justin did his best to paint a fair and honest picture of his childhood. 'I mean, some people have it misconstrued,' he began. 'I wasn't poor. I definitely didn't think of myself as *not* having a lot of money. But I definitely did not have a *lot* of money. I couldn't afford to get a lot of new clothes a lot of times. But I had a roof over my head. I was very fortunate. I had my grandparents, I saw them a lot, they were very kind. So I grew up getting everything that I wanted.'

Pattie loved Justin and wanted the best for him in life. A deeply religious woman, she prayed to God every day, asking Him to allow her son to succeed. She took Justin to church most weekends and he was quickly aware of the sense of belonging that churchgoers can find. He came from a small, two-person family but when he stepped inside their local church he would discover an extended family in the shape of its congregation, which brought him added and much-needed warmth and emotional security. It did the same for his mother, who found she could do with more of both these things herself.

Most significantly, Justin loved the music that was part of every church service. Pattie sang in a church band and her young boy was mesmerized by the hymns and joyful tunes that resonated around the church during services. Pattie had dreams of performing in other ways too. Growing up, her ambition had been to become an actress, but those aspirations were put on hold once she became not just a mother, but a single mother.

As she has recalled since, it was a real struggle for her to keep herself and Justin fed, clothed and housed. 'We were living below the poverty line,' said Pattie, somewhat contesting Justin's memories of the time. 'We had a roof over our heads and we had food in the house, but we struggled.' To keep them afloat she had to work extremely hard. 'I worked two jobs just to make ends meet,' she said. 'But we had all the essentials.'

Occasionally, her parents, Bruce and Diane Dale, would help out with some much-needed funds, as well as regular moral support. Diane was part of the Stratford establishment, working as a custodian in the municipal headquarters, though she has since retired.

Someone who observed Justin closely from an early age is Chad Ritter, a guy who acted as an unofficial 'big brother' figure to the young boy. Ritter befriended Pattie as Justin was growing up and therefore was able to observe the future pop sensation at close hand during his formative years. Ritter would drive to Stratford at the weekends to help entertain Justin. They went bowling, played pool and Laser Quest. Fun times for both of them. Ritter said Justin was 'a little bit of a smart aleck, a comedian, a jokester, a class clown sort of kid. He likes to get a reaction, to mess around.'

He described Justin's living arrangements as rather humble. 'They lived in a basement apartment, two bedrooms, in a big complex on the back-end part of Stratford,' said Ritter. 'His mom was kind of struggling. She didn't have full-time work. She couldn't always afford stuff for Justin.' However, Ritter insists that this was ultimately to Justin's advantage in one sense. 'I think the financial and living situation definitely helped Justin grow up a little quicker, because he started out with nothing. You can't get the average kid to understand the responsibilities or do what he does.'

Somehow, Pattie and Justin got by, but they were rarely more than comfortable at best. 'I grew up with not a lot of money,' Justin said. 'We never owned a house.' Although he was aware that they were at the poorer end of the riches scale, Justin speaks with fondness of his early years, which he described as 'A regular kid life – pretty normal'. From the start, though, he seemed destined to be anything but regular or normal. Pattie's daily prayers for Justin were that he would one day become a modern-day version of the biblical prophet Samuel, who had been a voice to his generation. She even hoped Justin might become a youth pastor, or that he might record religious songs for a Christian record label.

Soon after his birth, Justin began to show signs of a musical future. It all started during those Sunday-morning church services. 'I would just, like, play on the [organ] keys and stuff,' Justin remembered. 'People would show me stuff and I would try and do what they did. I just liked music, I really had a passion for music.' It is a passion that he seemed destined to fulfil from the beginning.

On the day Justin was born the pop charts were being dominated by diva singer Mariah Carey. In Britain she was at Number 1 in both the singles and album charts. The year 1994 was also a momentous one for world events. Nelson Mandela became the first black leader of South Africa; a huge earthquake hit Los Angeles, killing twenty people; in Britain the Channel Tunnel connecting England and France was opened. In show business, one of the biggest stories of the year was the marriage of American pop star Michael Jackson to the daughter of rock'n'roll legend Elvis Presley, Lisa Marie.

Of course, Justin was just a baby when these events took place, but as his love of music grew in subsequent years he quickly became a convert to Jackson's material, which had a big impact on him. Two of his favourite albums of all time are *Thriller* and *Bad*, which Jackson released in the 1980s, before Justin was even born. Both are such classic collections of infectious pop songs that they continue to be popular among people who were not alive when they were first released. Between them these albums have now sold around 100 million copies – somewhere among that total are the copies bought by Justin, who always loves the thrill of buying a new album.

People have sometimes compared the early career of Jackson with Justin's first steps in the industry. Certainly the tender age at which they became famous means there are similarities. However, while Justin first became known in his teenage years, Jackson was just eleven when the Jackson 5 released their first single in 1968. Justin was fifteen when he first released a song – an old-timer in comparison!

But he has been hugely influenced by Jackson. 'I was very inspired by him in his past,' said Justin, who rejected the suggestion that he is too young to understand the legacy left by Jackson. 'I definitely do understand it,' he said. 'Like, I grew up listening to Michael a lot. My mum listened to him and I watched him on YouTube; I still watch him on YouTube. I do understand what a great artist he was and that he really influenced pop.' As well as enjoying Jackson's songs, Justin also loved those of the soul legend Stevie Wonder, who began his own career on the same Motown label as Jackson.

The first song he loved was, he said, '"God is Bigger Than the Boogie Man" from [the animated series] *VeggieTales*. And when I was, like, seven or six, Boyz II Men's "On Bended Knee". My mom used to play the album over and over. I would go to my bedroom and try to do the vocal acrobatics.'

While Justin has been inspired by some artists, including Jackson, he is clear that he has always tried to stay true to himself and choose his own path. 'I had people I looked up to,' he said of those days, 'but I would never try to be like anybody.' He added, 'I've learnt a lot from listening to Michael Jackson and Boyz II Men, though.'

One of Justin's favourite Jackson songs is 'I'll Be There', which was released in 1970. The sweet promises of loyalty and devotion in the lyrics are much the same as those in some of Justin's own songs, and Justin has performed the track beautifully with his guitar. However, as he said, he was never a big fan of any particular pop act as a child and perhaps because of this he has at times found his fans' hysterical reactions to him a little confusing to deal with.

Justin is most famed for his smooth, sweet voice but his top fans know that he plays a number of instruments well. He learned to play the drums, he says, at the age of two and was able at that very tender age – when most kids are still perfecting the art of walking and talking – to play a convincing 'four-four' beat. This was not on an actual drum kit, though. He improvised by hitting the beats on household items like cushions, pots and pans. It was not until he was four that Pattie, impressed by her young son's ability with the sticks and tiring of him hitting the furniture, bought him his first ever real drum kit.

Drum kits do not come cheap, but the local church helped out with the cost of it. Indeed, a collection had been undertaken at the church specifically to fund the purchase. The parishioners could not have known they were funding the development of a boy who would, little over a decade later, become a global pop sensation.

To make sure that Justin would not disturb the family's

neighbours with his practising, his grandparents agreed that he could keep the drum kit in their cellar and bash away at it there, where only minimal disturbance would be caused. The location was not the only issue to be resolved for Justin's new pastime. He is left-handed but the drum kit was constructed – as most are – for a right-handed player. To complicate the lessons more, his teachers (who were the drummers from the church's choir band) were also right-handed, which made it even more tricky for Justin to learn from them.

He has always been a determined boy so he overcame these obstacles and became a very impressive drummer. A video on his YouTube channel shows how great he was on the drums from an early age. In the short video he is shown bashing away brilliantly at a friend's drum kit, playing set, steady beats, adding in some drum rolls and also displaying a fine hand on the cymbals. Most impressive of all is how at ease he seems as he plays. The video truly shows he was born to perform music. He was soon playing very well indeed and his natural musical skill was already gaining him admirers.

With his skill on the drums growing, Justin was in no mood to stop his musical development, and went on to teach himself to play a range of other musical instruments, including piano, guitar and trumpet. 'I guess you can say I've been blessed with talent,' he said.

He comes from what he describes as a 'somewhat musically inclined' family. His grandmother is a talented pianist who is, he says, 'a great singer, and stuff'. As we'll see, she also wrote her own songs, and one of them was included in the early YouTube uploads made on the Internet site that launched him to global superstardom.

Justin's father is a guitar player and singer, but the boy's first guitar was a hand-me-down given to him by his mother when he was six. She had bought new strings for it and lovingly restrung it before handing it over to Justin, who, of course, plays guitar left-handed. He was dwarfed by the instrument and was a picture of cuteness when, as a young kid, he peered over the top of the guitar body while strumming away.

He had picked up the basics of drumming himself and followed the same self-taught path in the early days with his guitar. This was no ordinary boy: Justin's dedication was extraordinary. 'He wasn't always an amazing guitar player,' said Chad Ritter. 'He picked it up and worked at it. He pushes himself – there's a competitive edge.'

Justin concentrated hard as he picked up chords and his focus on guitar-playing remains strong to this very day. 'When I play guitar and someone's trying to talk to me I'm just zoned out,' he says. Occasionally, a friend of his mother would pop by the apartment to teach Justin a bit more on the guitar and he always picked it up quickly.

One of the first songs he learned to play on the guitar was 'Wheat Kings' by a Canadian rock band called The Tragically Hip. It is a moving ballad that touches on the story of a Canadian man who was wrongly convicted of a crime. Whenever Justin has performed this very maturely themed song, including during television and radio interviews, he has taken it on with ease and grace.

How did this fine, natural talent emerge so early? 'I just

grew up around music my whole life,' he said. From morning to night, he never stopped being musical. 'I would just sing around the house,' he wrote on his MySpace website page. 'It was just kind of a thing that I loved to do.' Even as he brushed his teeth before bed, Justin would be singing pop songs.

'When he was five, he'd hear something on the radio and go to the keyboard and figure it out,' recalled his proud mother. His bedroom walls were plastered with big posters of his musical heroes, including the American R&B boy band Boyz II Men, a band that had been formed at high school and found fame young, in the same way as Justin would. Not that fame was on Justin's mind in his earliest years. He was too busy enjoying himself. 'I would always just sing around the house and play instruments, but I never tried to get famous,' he said.

However, he did have in mind a possible future route to stardom, although he initially favoured a sporting route rather than a musical one. 'I sang, but it was just for fun,' he said. 'I did a lot of different stuff. I played sports. Singing was just another hobby . . . And I never took it seriously. I never got lessons. I use to practise my signature for hockey. It's kind of how I learned to give my autograph.'

His sporting hero was Canadian ice-hockey star Wayne Gretzky, who is widely considered the greatest ever player in that sport. 'I played hockey a lot,' Justin said of his earlier years. 'I was really focused on sports.' Like lots of Canadian kids, Justin also enjoyed following ice-hockey teams, including the local side, the Cullitons, and the Toronto Maple Leafs. Since becoming famous he has said that his favourite alternative career would be playing hockey in the National Hockey League.

That said, there's another career path that also appeals to him. 'If I wasn't a pop star I'd be a chef,' he said. 'I would cook all the lovely ladies a nice dinner.' If he was to take such a path there would be no shortage of willing diners. He has also spoken of an earlier interest in becoming an architect, so Justin is clearly not a boy who has lacked ambition.

He really enjoyed taking part in sporting and athletic activities. Justin played hockey and soccer with more enthusiasm than skill: he was once described as a 'scrappy' athlete. His ever-protective mother was more upbeat, saying: 'He's always been very gifted at pretty much everything he does.'

His grandfather said that sporting activity was essential for Justin, who had been blessed with bundles of energy. 'He's always been energetic. You had to keep him going all the time. He had to be in sports all the time, or if not, he was bouncing off the walls.'

A girl who claimed she was at kindergarten with him remembers Justin as a cheeky and hyperactive kid. 'She said he was always in trouble, wouldn't sit still,' the girl's grandmother said, 'the class clown'.

However, Justin insisted he was 'home schooled' by his mother between kindergarten and grade 1. That said, he readily admits that he is always full of life and that he enjoys being in the middle of the action. 'I like to goof off and be the centre of attention,' he has said.

Occasional high bursts of energy are one of the attributes

often linked with Pisceans like Justin. People born under that star sign are also believed to be keen on connecting with the world. Justin would fulfil that in time, but for now he enjoyed more low-key pastimes including playing chess, and he showed his tactical mind when he won tournaments as a child.

The first school he attended was the Jeanne Sauvé Catholic School on Grange Street in Stratford. It was here that he took his elementary grades. Jeanne Sauvé is a French immersion school in which religion is an important part of the curriculum. Indeed, as the school's promotional material boasts, its education is 'rooted in our faith in Jesus Christ'. During his time there, Justin learned to speak fluent French, which during interviews he has since impressively demonstrated. He can also count to ten in German, after being taught to do so by his German great-grandfather.

He moved on to the Stratford Northwestern Public School on Forman Avenue. His favourite high-school teacher was called Mr Montheith. 'He gave me a lot of slack,' remembered Justin. 'I gave teachers a hard time sometimes.'

Mr Montheith recalled that Justin was a boy full of spirit and endeavour. 'He has no fear, is one of the things that I found about him,' said the teacher. 'I couldn't believe how quickly he could pick things up, whether it be basketball, soccer, or obviously, music and dancing and that sort of stuff.'

Another of Justin's favourite teachers from school was Miss Brooker, who also noticed his musical potential. 'I remember recognizing Justin's passion for singing even in grade 7,' she said. 'My favorite subjects are probably, like, English,' said Justin. 'I don't really like math.' He has said that he quite enjoyed algebra, though.

Like most boys, as a schoolboy Justin had an eye for girls and claims that even before he became famous he had 'a lot of girls chasing me'. He dated a few, starting when he was around thirteen years old, and remembers that his first kiss came around that time. It happened during a school dance, but he does not remember the name of the lucky girl. The kiss was, he said, 'cool', but he added, 'I told my friends, I said, "the first person to kiss a girl gets $10". And so, my boys – they didn't kiss anyone. They said, "Justin, you should do it!" I was slow-dancing with this girl and then I just went in!'

He confirmed that the girl 'went with it', even though, as he put it, 'back then I was just some regular hockey-playing kid, so I was lucky that she kissed me back'. Fun times, but these early romantic experiences were nothing particularly serious. He said of his first girlfriend that they were not together for long. 'A month later, we broke up. I had that little stomach pain for a couple of days, but then I was cool.' He also remembered that one girl he asked out at school turned him down. 'You know, it was one of those little crushes you have when you're younger,' he told *US Weekly*. 'I asked her out and she said no.'

In fact, some of his schoolday experiences are surprising given what a teen icon he has become. With money so tight at home Justin was not always kitted out in the trendiest of clothes. He had to make do with what Pattie could afford to buy for him. This, combined with his short stature, made him an easy target for teasing from bullies. Naturally, this upset him and Pattie turned to a male friend of hers to have an encouraging word with the youngster.

The remarkable way in which Justin has risen from a target of schoolroom teasing to become one of the most popular teenagers on the planet is surely an inspiration to anyone who is targeted that way.

Some of the teasing was more playful and harmless. One day a classmate of Justin's played a practical joke on him. Justin had worked on a project that involved him giving a presentation to the class. As he stood up to give his presentation, the whole class began to laugh at him. At first he could not work out what had happened.

Only a little later did he realize that it was because one of his classmates had drawn an amusing picture on the project Justin was presenting. It was certainly a red-faced moment for Justin when he realized what had happened, but there were no hard feelings. Indeed, the two boys are friends to this day.

Nobody was about to tease Justin when they watched him dance, though. From an early age he took bust some impressive moves and a short video clip of an eight-year-old Justin break-dancing shows what skill he had on the dance floor even as a young schoolboy.

The last school he attended was the Stratford Northwestern Secondary School, where he took his grades 9–12. It was on the same campus as the Public School, and Justin could walk from the campus to the Rotary Arena on Glastonbury Drive, which was the venue for his Rotary house-league hockey games as a child. The Rotary Arena has since been upstaged by a brand new Rotary Complex. Across town are two other venues where Justin played hockey and soccer. The first is the William Allman Memorial Arena on Morenz Drive. He played for a travel hockey team in this historic building and loved the thrill of sporting competition with his friends. He found it a great way to get closer to people and build friendships, though naturally there were tensions between players as well. Justin played soccer for a travel soccer team called the Stratford Strikers, a team he thanked in the sleeve notes of his debut album, *My World*. These games were fierce and sweaty affairs that were played out on the Cooper Standard Soccer Fields on Packham Road.

Justin began to be noticed while playing at the under-eleven level. On one Friday night in June 2004 his team beat Taxandria 8–4. The healthy win was all the more impressive given that Taxandria had taken the lead. Justin was key to his team's comeback and was the best player on the field. He set off on some mazy runs into the opposition's penalty area and scored twice. No wonder he kept his place in the team as he grew older.

In one game, against another under-thirteen team called London United Fury, Justin was where he loves to be: right in the centre of the action.

The scoring began with a free kick, which Nolan Murray fired in from 20 yards out. Justin was then fouled in the penalty area, earning his side a spot kick, which his teammate Tyler Strawbridge nervously stepped up to take. Thankfully he scored with the penalty and he celebrated with Justin. Later in the game, Zach Bandura fed the ball to Justin who made no mistake with his shot and scored himself, capping a fine victory for the Strikers.

He has always been a short boy for his age but Justin never let this intimidate him on the field. Against London City Titans White he and his teammate Ryan Butler were dwarfed by their opposite numbers but carried on bravely. They managed to intimidate their opponents and create a number of chances for their team. However, you can't win them all – the match ended 0–0.

Win, lose or draw, Justin loved to compete on the football field. Those were happy times for him and his teammates and they all created a close bond as a team. Thanks to his ever-enthusiastic nature, Justin was a particularly popular figure in the team, and after a game he and the other players would walk together to the Scoopers ice-cream bar on Erie Street for a hard-earned treat. After burning off so many calories in those sweat-soaked games they had plenty of room for ice cream and soft drinks, which always tasted so much the nicer after seventy minutes on the football field.

But even if the fun had left him breathless, Justin was soon back on his usual bouncy form, making his buddies laugh, and they would all look forward to the next game when the fun could continue. He might be a solo artist now but back in those days he showed that he is a great team player both on and off the pitch. 'I think it's really important to have your close friends around you,' he says. Nowadays he loves the team that follows him on the road – and many of them have said they consider themselves a family now.

When the weather was good Justin also liked to play on the streets with his friends. He loved his skateboard and worked hard on his boarding skills at Stratford Skate Park, which sits in the shadow of the town's YMCA building on St Patrick Street. On a pleasant day there he and his pals had great fun as they compared skateboarding tricks and competed with each other, but always in a friendly atmosphere. As he has since shown on videos uploaded to YouTube and photographs published by *Teen Vogue* magazine, he was a handy skateboarder. Among the tricks he can perform impressively are the '360', the 'Ollie' and the 'kickflip'.

He was also often spotted at the YMCA building itself, where he was enrolled in its daycare scheme. He has even been seen back there since finding fame and moving away to America. More competition between him and his pals took place at a hang-out called the Pour House, just round the corner from the park. This venue used to be called Sid's Pub but was changed into a pool hall, and Justin loved challenging his friends to a few frames of the game there. He was always delighted to win but tried to be a good sport whatever the outcome.

All that competing made Justin a hungry boy as he grew

up. In common with many other Northwestern pupils, he enjoyed stopping by the Madelyn's Diner on Huron Street for breakfast before heading into class. It is a popular spot in the mornings, drawing hungry customers from many miles around for its unrivalled breakfasts, omelettes being a particular favourite.

Justin was also a fairly regular face at another establishment called Features, where he loved the breakfast menu. One of the more ambitious dishes served in the morning was the Paul Bunyan platter, which included eggs, bacon, French toast, fluffy pancakes and potatoes. It was named after a mythical giant lumberjack and while a giant could comfortably tuck away such a huge platter, it was more than a boy Justin's age could easily manage.

For lunch, Justin was a regular at the Subway outlet on Huron Street. He loves the Subway sandwiches, soft drinks and other fast-food staples that are on offer at the famous chain. Even now he has found fame Justin still loves a Subway treat when his schedule allows. Sometimes he would return to Madelyn's in the evening with his mother who rated the eatery, run by Madelyn Carty, as her favourite restaurant in the area. At night it takes on the atmosphere of a traditional American diner straight from the 1950s, with its burgers, fries, onion rings and milkshakes.

Justin loves pasta, too. One of his favourite dishes is spaghetti bolognese, and for dessert he thinks you can't do better than a good old apple pie. He enjoys pouring himself an orange juice to accompany his meal, whatever the time of day. If he was arranging an ideal romantic evening for a girl he would want to be doing the cooking himself, 'I'd probably make her a steak dinner,' he said.

Although he tries to eat healthily whenever he can, Justin admits that one of his habits is 'eating too much candy'. His favourites are the Sour Patch Kids chewy sweets.

In the morning, at home, breakfast isn't breakfast without the popular cereal Cap'n Crunch, and he's also fond of the world-renowned Canadian treat of pancakes with maple syrup. He has also been known to tuck into a cheesecake, his favourite type being cherry. He believes the best kind of chocolates to give a girl as a present are Hershey's Kisses. These chocolates were first launched way back in 1907, and have since become a popular romantic gesture, including special Valentine's Day editions.

At the weekend, Justin liked to go to the Festival Marketplace, on the outskirts of Stratford. There is a shop there called Long & McQuade Music Store, where he would often be seen on a Saturday. Across the road from the Marketplace is the King's Buffet. This was the setting for a historic moment in any boy's life: his first ever date with a girl.

'I like taking a girl out for dinner and buying her flowers,' the romantic Justin has said. But his first date went far from smoothly. 'We'd go out for dinner,' said Justin, when asked how a perfect romantic evening would work. 'An ideal first date is basically for me to make the girl feel happy.'

Sadly, this was not to be an ideal date. He was nervous on the night and after starting reasonably well the evening turned into a disaster when he accidentally spilt spaghetti and meatballs all over himself. 'She never went out with me again,' he revealed of the unnamed girl. Little could she have known at the time that she was passing up the chance to date the boy who would within a few years become a global pin-up and one of the most desired teenagers on the planet. Girls across the globe would now be ecstatically happy to date Justin – whether he spilt his food over himself or not!

There are no hard feelings on his side. 'She was really nice,' he remembered of his first date. However, he still sometimes has a little cringe when he remembers how badly the evening went. 'It was terrible and embarrassing,' he said. Ever one to look on the bright side, he has lived and learned. 'So I would suggest *not* going out for Italian on a first date because it can be messy! I'll never make that mistake again!'

Another unpleasant experience he had as a child was the scary day when he was stuck in a lift for four hours. It was a traumatic experience with each minute he was trapped seeming to take much longer to pass by. 'They had to call people two hours away to come and fix it,' he recalled.

Finally, the engineers arrived and freed poor Justin from the cramped lift. It was a terrible experience for anyone to go through, let alone a young boy. Understandably, the memory of it continues to haunt him to this day. 'I'm very claustrophobic and scared of elevators,' he has said. He will now often take stairs or an escalator rather than a lift.

As the mania around him has grown, he has been forced to get used to fans mobbing him. 'I'm a really claustrophobic person to begin with,' he told *Maclean's*. 'I hate elevators, especially crammed elevators. I get really scared. So I think that it's very definitely scary when girls are all around me and I can't go anywhere. At the same time, I guess I've got to get used to it, you know what I mean?' Another of Justin's fears is the dark, and he likes to sleep with at least some light in the room.

Justin has always loved to read, ever since his mother taught him how to as a child. Growing up, his favourite book was called *We're Going on a Bear Hunt*, by British author Michael Rosen, and illustrated by Helen Oxenbury. It follows the experiences of a family who embark on a 'bear hunt': they walk through grass, mud and a river in search of the elusive animal – and encounter a surprise when they enter a cave.

The book is popular around the world among children and adults, and it was written to appeal to anyone from three years of age or older. For Justin, it was a joyful story and one that particularly appealed to his sense of adventure and fun. The approach the family in the story take to obstacles is the same as the one Justin has taken in his own life. As they reach the river, the dark forest and other obstacles, they realize there is no avoiding them: they have to go through it. Each time, they manage to overcome the hurdle life has thrown at them. Perhaps when life has tested Justin he too has realized: I've got to go through it.

As well as enjoying reading Justin is also a fan of movies. He loves the 1976 film *Rocky*, which stars Sylvester Stallone. It is the story of a down-and-out fighter who is given the unlikely opportunity to fight for the world championship. Although the title character is a fine boxer, he seems to have lost his chance to compete and to be destined to live in disappointment and poverty. Then, a publicity stunt arranged by a friend gives him a shot at the big time. He still has to work hard and be brave, but he finally gets the chance to make it and rise from his humble surroundings. No wonder Justin loved the film – the story has many similarities to his own life! He also enjoys the heroic film *Saving Private Ryan*, which is set in the Second World War and stars Tom Hanks and Matt Damon.

However, Justin also loves cuter films like the animated Disney film *Cars* and the street-dancing comedy movie *You Got Served* (the dancing competition of the plot probably reminds him of the Stratford Star contest in which he took part). The head-to-head between two drummers in another of Justin's favourite films, *Drumline*, and the dance showcase in the 2006 movie *Step Up* probably also remind him of the Stratford Star days.

Asked what his favourite girlie movie is he chose *The Notebook*. Here, an elderly man narrates the long story of a romance he had enjoyed during his life. But this is not the only girlie movie Justin has watched and liked. *A Walk to Remember* is a teen romance film that was released in 2002. Justin loves this film, and its soundtrack, too.

From cartoons to uplifting romance stories and movies about people rising from humble beginnings, Justin is a great film fan, and he loves watching TV as well, including the Superman-based series *Smallville* and the American medical drama series *Grey's Anatomy. American Idol,* the successful reality pop series that featured the famous and straight-talking British judge Simon Cowell for its first nine series, is another favourite.

Since finding fame, Justin has moved from Canada to live in America. His success has brought him an enviable lifestyle, which means he regularly travels the world to promote his music and meet his fans. He has to work hard to meet all the demands thrown at him but all the same, it is the sort of life that many people dream about. He will always remain the sweet boy from Canada, though, because for Justin home really is where the heart is. 'I've been to a lot of places around the world,' he said, 'but my favourite place is still my home town.'

He is a proud Canadian who loved everything about life in the country, including the heavy snowfalls that often came with the winter. Indeed, when he travelled to Britain during the snowy winter of 2010 he was amused by how the country struggled to deal with the snow. As a Canadian he is accustomed to a far more efficient approach to extreme weather, and remembers with some fondness the cold winters there. He expressed his surprise on his Twitter page and was asked about this during an interview with the Digital Spy website. 'You guys are acting like it's the end of the world – everything's cancelled and the subway's not working – but in Canada this is, like, the least amount of snow we get,' he said. 'We have to have at least ten inches of snow to get a day off school.'

Justin was asked what advice he, as a Canadian, would offer the British about dealing with snowfall. 'Hmm . . . let me think . . . well, for a start, you guys aren't wearing the right sort of clothes. You need to wear hats, scarves, mitts . . . and long johns! I always wear long johns when it's cold. I know they're not cool but I'd rather be warm than cold.'

Better to be warm than cold, even if that means not being cool, then, Justin?

Now he is famous, Justin loves travelling the world and keeps his millions of fans updated on his latest movements via his ever-popular Twitter feed. But for him personally his most memorable trip came before he was even famous. It was a holiday to remember for Justin and his mother. What was most amazing about it was that Justin, then just a thirteen-year-old boy, had funded the entire trip himself. Bursting with initiative, love and dedication, he had found a way to thank his mother for all she had done for him. Unsurprisingly, music was at the heart of his remarkable initiative, which was the first big sign that Justin had the sort of qualities that could make him a star.

2

A Busking Boy

ustin is a bright and loving boy who has always been grateful for the many sacrifices his mother made on his behalf. He watched in wonderment as she worked round the clock to keep them both fed, clothed and housed. Although he could not be aware of all the luxuries she went without in order to support him, he knew she was going without many things. She had been particularly supportive of his musical ambitions, doing her best to help him acquire instruments and take lessons. He never became in any way spoilt by her love and attention. On the contrary, Justin was determined to find a way to repay her for all she had done for him.

It's not easy for a thirteen-year-old to earn money, particularly to raise enough for the plan he had in mind. So he had a good think about how he could do this, and hatched a plan he hoped might work . . . He strapped his outsized guitar around his shoulders and marched out onto the streets of Stratford to busk.

Like most buskers he found a nice busy spot, put his guitar case at his feet so passers-by had somewhere to drop their money, and began playing and singing in the hope he could serenade the public into parting with a couple of dollars.

He originally started busking to raise money for a very different reason. 'I wanted to go golfing with my friends and I didn't have money, so I went out [to perform],' he remembered. But once he realized what a success he could make of busking, he set his sights higher. One photograph shows him sitting on some marble stairs. He is wearing a blue baseball cap, a yellow T-shirt, white hooded jumper, blue jeans and blue trainers. He has a bottle of water at his side and his guitar case at his feet. It already holds a decent collection of notes and coins.

Thanks to a stroke of luck, a video of one of his busking sessions does exist. A group of school pupils were on a day trip to Stratford when they walked past the theatre. There they saw young Justin singing enthusiastically and they decided to film him – having no idea that this was a future star, they were just enjoying his performance.

Among the songs he sang while they filmed was 'I'll Be' by Edwin McCain. He also performed 'Refine Me' by Jennifer Knapp, a song that was close to his heart thanks to its religious themes. It is clear from the video that the assembled crowd were enjoying his performance and many photographs were shot. The enjoyment was obviously shared by the performer, who always seemed to display his trademark sunny temperament.

'He liked being with people and entertaining,' said Chad Ritter of Justin as a child. 'I always believed in him. It's one of those things where either you've got it or you don't – and Justin has just got it.'

And it wasn't just passers-by who took notice of him. He was quickly spotted by Eldon Gammon, the house manager of the Avon Theatre outside which Justin did most of his busking. Gammon remembered Justin as the 'little guy with the big voice' – a description that has been used many times since. 'It almost seemed like the guitar was bigger than him,' Gammon told *The Toronto Star*.

However, the boy was also an arresting performer and often became a strong rival to the theatre's production. 'Student groups, they poured around him. The five-minute call would go – it's an announcement that you could hear all over – and then we would have to drag them away from him. He had a good persona with people. He was always very polite, always said "Thank you." It's interesting that the music he's doing now is nothing like what he did here.'

The music has changed but Justin's polite yet charismatic personality continues to charm fans around the world, just as it did in Stratford back in his busking days.

Justin remembers those days very fondly. A few years later he returned to the site with a television crew. 'This is, like, one of the main tourist attractions, so there's always a bunch of people out here,' he told them when they arrived at the location. 'I sang "I'll Be" by Edwin McCain, "You and Me" by Lifehouse, "U Got It Bad" by Usher and "Cry Me a River",' he recalled. 'I'd make $200. I would play outside, and I would put out my guitar case, and people would, like, throw me any change and stuff,' he said.

The figure of $200 is all the more impressive when you realize that he made that amount in just one hour. 'Very seldom did he come home from a night without $150 to $200 for sitting there for about an hour,' recalled his grandmother. The hourly totals soon added up to a healthy sum of money. 'I made three thousand dollars and I took my mum on vacation to Florida,' he smiled. 'Yeah, it was pretty awesome.' Awesome indeed.

Pattie was the proudest and happiest mother in the world as she and Justin packed their bags and set off for Florida. It was the first proper holiday Justin and his mother had ever enjoyed and it became a trip to remember. 'He took us on our first vacation ever,' Pattie said. 'We went to Disneyland.'

It was the trip of a lifetime for them, and nobody could have been prouder than his mother, whom Justin has always described as his favourite person in the whole world. She knew that the trip was a gesture of love from her son, who had worked so hard to make sure they could take it. Not many children the age Justin was then would have been so enterprising.

Where did this astonishing sense of purpose and determination come from? Justin credits his mother with some of it. Certainly the way she worked during his upbringing set a fine example to him. He also feels his humble upbringing helped shape him positively too. 'I grew up below the poverty line,' he said. 'I didn't have as much as other people did. I think it made me stronger as a person – it built my character.' The way Justin has taken the tests that life has thrown at him and turned them to his own advantage is an inspirational example to everyone.

Meanwhile, Justin's musical development continued. At the age of thirteen he picked up and learned to play the trumpet; he also continued to sing around the house. Whatever he was doing, whatever he was wearing, whatever time of day it was, Justin's sweet voice could be heard. He began to sing with the church choir, too. In a way these were the first ever Justin Bieber concerts – although they were held in a church, not a concert hall or theatre! Many people who heard him sing remarked that he had a special voice and enjoyed his sweet and harmonious tone. Once you added in his cute face and lovable personality, you had the full package, which mesmerized people from the start.

At the same time, Justin's confidence as a singer was growing. Having already captured people's imagination as a busker and then a choir singer, Justin was about to take a whole new step in his musical ambitions.

However, while he had admirers, Justin is not sure of when he himself first truly realized he had a special talent for singing. 'I don't know if I remember,' he told the website neonlimelight.com when asked which of the songs he sang was the one he felt really showed him how great his voice was. 'I think maybe "So Sick" by Ne-Yo.'

The artist Ne-Yo (real name Shaffer Chimere Smith) is an R&B star who has worked with British *X Factor* winners Leona Lewis and Alexandra Burke. He released his debut album *In My Own Words* in 2006, and the stand-out track was 'So Sick', which reached Number 1 in America when he released it as a single. Justin loved the song, which suited his voice well. It was to form part of his next move musically, one that eventually propelled him to fame and fortune.

The boy with the angelic voice was ready to go to a new level – and to compete with other singers. The contest took place more or less on his own doorstep. 'Stratford Star' (sometimes referred to as 'Stratford Idol') is a singing competition that now takes place in the town once a year. It is held at the YMCA building and typically runs for between three and four weeks. Posters advertising the contest are placed in schools around the area.

The contest was first run in 2006, and when Justin heard about it he thought it would be a great thing to take part in. So the following year Justin decided he really had to sign up. The way the contest is organized is similar to reality-television programmes like *The X Factor* and *American Idol*. After some nerve-racking initial auditions, a top ten of the best singers was chosen.

As Justin has explained since, he approached the contest in a very different way to all his fellow contestants. 'The other people in the competition had been taking singing lessons and had vocal coaches,' he said. 'I wasn't taking it too seriously at times,' he added. Most of all, he simply wanted to enjoy himself. 'I just did it for fun, I wasn't trying to be famous or anything.'

However, local people remember Justin taking it a bit more seriously than that. Angie Adair, who helped arrange Stratford Star, remembers him using the YMCA centre's karaoke machine to practise. Sometimes he was practising so hard and for so long that she had to ask him to leave so she could close the centre.

The fun he was having was clear from the first time he sang onstage in the competition. The song he had chosen was 'Angel' by Sarah McLachlan. He stood casually by the microphone stand, wearing a cap back to front and singing the words as the pianist accompanied him. The song is about an angel and Justin sang just like one. 'Angel' also has a sad and grown-up theme but when Justin sang it he brought out the beauty and the sweet side of the piece . . .

He was through to the next round!

'Show Justin Bieber some respect!' said the compère as she introduced him for his next song. The audience began to cheer and scream and the compère added, 'Justin's singing "Respect"'.

He was wearing a brown baseball cap back to front, a grey checked shirt, brown trousers and large trainers. As he took the microphone in his left hand he looked a little nervous, but as soon as the track began he danced happily around the stage – even managing to pull off a few twists and twirls as he danced. He sang the song well, with a rather high-pitched delivery. At times, his voice seemed to belong to someone much older and more experienced than him. To put his own stamp on the song he threw in some extra touches, like chanting 'Come on!' between lines.

When it came to the part in the song where the singer takes a break and a saxophone solo takes the lead, Justin was in no mood simply to rest. He held an imaginary saxophone and mimed the solo, like a wannabe guitarist would play 'air guitar'. Here he brought huge personality and cute naughtiness to the stage, as he 'played along' cheekily, much to the delight of the audience – and his time at home learning the trumpet seemed to pay off when it came to him miming with an imaginary saxophone.

At one stage he got so caught up in the fun of his playful miming that he accidentally dropped the microphone. As it hit the stage it sent a loud thud through the speaker system, but he quickly picked it up and carried on his performance.

Despite his toying around during the instrumental section, Justin showed great maturity and professionalism in his vocal technique. Often amateur singers make the mistake of singing with their mouths too close to the microphone. Not Justin. He held the microphone the correct distance from his mouth and when he was singing a louder note he moved it a bit further away, before returning it to a closer position for the softer notes.

As he sang and danced he looked so happy. The stage was lit up by flashbulbs from photographers in the audience. When he neared the end of the song he added in a 'That's all I want!' after the backing track chanted 'Respect!'. He was certainly getting plenty of that from the audience, particularly when he drew out the closing note with real soul. The audience cheered, screamed and clapped again.

Justin was on a natural high by this stage and punched the air in celebration. He then handed the microphone back to the compère and for a moment appeared unsure about what to do. Looking a little sheepish, he tucked his hands in his pockets. His modest body language was in contrast to the star performance he had just put in, which suggested that the added confidence he felt while singing partly left him once he stopped doing so. Either way, it was hard to believe that the boy on the stage was only thirteen.

When he returned to the stage to sing 'Fallin'' by Alicia Keys, Justin was much more smartly dressed. He had a light blue shirt and a dark blue tie. Even though he had entered the contest mostly to have fun, he was also clearly taking it more seriously as the proceedings went on. He did wear the shirt outside his dark trousers, though, which brought a little informality to the look.

'All right! Next we will hear from Justin Bieber,' said the compère. 'Come on up and we'll hear "Fallin'".' The song begins with vocals, before the music kicks in. Justin sang the opening note well, with a raspy edge to his voice that again made him sound more mature and experienced than he actually was. He added a soulful side to the song by laying his palm flat against his chest during the bigger notes.

This was a polished performer who had clearly studied the stage ways of the top musical stars. As he finished the song the audience screamed and applauded. 'Thank you,' he said sweetly. The compère took the microphone back and told Justin his performance had been 'fantastic', adding, 'I think Alicia Keys would be a bit jealous of that one.'

It was a more confident and energetic Justin who returned to sing the uplifting song '3 a.m.' written by Rob Thomas, the singer in a band called Matchbox Twenty.

'Take it away,' said the compère – and Justin did just that. 'Hey everybody,' he said to the audience, leading them in overhead clapping. In between the verses he encouraged the audience to clap along. When the song came to an end he really drew out the final note once again.

As the audience began to clap, for a moment Justin clapped too. When the compère came to take the microphone back he half bowed to her. It had been an upbeat performance and he deserved every bit of the applause and praise that it drew. Justin left the stage on a natural high – he was truly loving the experience of performing in front of a live audience. And the audience? Well, they were enjoying the experience just as much!

He made it to the final three of the competition thanks to his performance of two more songs, including 'So Sick' by Ne-Yo. This time he began the performance with the microphone on its stand rather than holding it, and despite his small size he managed not to appear dwarfed by the stand, which he abandoned midway through the song. It was a somewhat low-key performance overall. Justin had his hand in his pocket at several points, bringing a casual edge to his formal shirt-and-tie outfit. He was standing directly underneath a portrait of Queen Elizabeth II at the time. For his second song in this stage Justin was dressed in a streetwise style that was more in keeping with the image we now have of him. He wore a baseball cap, a baggy jumper and jeans, together with the huge trainers again.

He encouraged the audience to clap as the song started and then performed some break-dancing moves, including a fine backspin that drew admiring noises from the crowd. 'Come on, yeah!' he said, throwing his baseball cap into the audience like a true star.

The song he was performing was 'Basketball' by Lil' Bow Wow, who himself began his career at just thirteen years of age. Justin danced cheekily throughout the song, pulling the hood of his jumper over his head at one point. His dancing was not quite of Michael Jackson quality, but for a boy of his age and level of experience it was wonderful. The audience showed its appreciation with cheers and whoops.

At the finale, it was very clear that Justin was competing against older rivals when he stood on stage next to the two contestants who joined him in the top three, for they towered above him. And forget that he had entered the contest mostly to have fun: now he had got this far Justin was keen to win, and he was understandably nervous as he waited for the winner to be announced. This might not have been as big a stage or audience as for *The X Factor* or *American Idol*, but for Justin at that moment it meant everything.

A different compère took to the stage to deliver the final judges' final verdict. She started with a jokey mention of how she felt a little uncomfortable to be the one delivering the news. 'So, of my fellow judges, I'm not sure why I get stuck doing the voting thing but that's okay!' She then turned to the three contestants and told them that they were 'all winners', regardless of who finished on top. She added: 'It takes so much to get up on stage to showcase a talent like that. I know that the crowds come out to see you every week and you've just done such a phenomenal performance every time, all of you. Please don't ever stop. Like I said to each of you on different occasions, it's so important and music is so important – so just keep singing, no matter what.'

She was leaving them hanging – all three contestants were desperate to hear who had won. Justin looked especially nervous, though he tried to cover his anxiety by putting his hands on his hips. The compère then turned to the audience, who cheered with excitement, knowing the final verdict was moments away.

'So,' she began, before giggling nervously as the tension continued to fill the hall. 'Okay, Emma's going to help me. She's going to pass the torch to our next Stratford Star winner – who this year is Kirsten Hawley!'

Justin was hugely disappointed not to win, but he showed great maturity in his response. He applauded as Kirsten was handed the prize and was the first to offer her a handshake of congratulation. He was little over half the height of the winner, but in the way he handled defeat he stood very tall.

'I have more things to say,' said the compère, once the cheering, screaming and applause had died down. 'All three contestants have actually been invited to sing at an autism [charity] benefit,' she explained, asking them to stay behind for five minutes so she could give them the details. She then handed Justin and the other runner-up a consolation prize.

While the audience showed its appreciation for the runners-up, the compère bent down to give Justin a hug. As all three walked off the stage at the end of the night it was strikingly clear once more how much shorter he was compared to his rivals.

Despite feeling crushed not to have won after he had performed so well, Justin continued to be graceful in defeat, and managed to smile cutely at the winner as he applauded her once more. Again, he smiled sweetly when another of the organizers told the contestants she realized how hard they had worked.

He might not have won the contest, but Justin had won many hearts. People who have finished as runners-up in talent contests have sometimes gone on to do as well as – or even better than – the winner. The boy-band JLS were disappointed when they finished runners-up to Alexandra Burke in the 2008 series of British reality-television show *The X Factor*. However, since then they have sold over a million albums and also won two prestigious BRIT Awards, leading some people to believe they did even better than the winner.

This was not a one-off occurrence: in the first series of *The X Factor* the runners-up, a band called G4, went on to outsell by far the winner, a gravel-voiced solo soul singer called Steve Brookstein. The same has happened in American and Canadian TV talent contests, so young Justin could take encouragement from how well he had done. As it has turned out, he might become the most successful runner-up ever!

In the wake of the contest Justin sang more and more. Much of this singing took place around the house but he also used his growing experience of performing onstage to his advantage by signing up for other local events.

In August 2007 he took part in a concert to tie in with an environment-awareness event known as the Virtual Blackout. Local residents were encouraged to switch off electrical items – lights, televisions, computers and suchlike – for a few hours to conserve energy. 'We need to make people aware of our dependence on energy,' said one of the organizers. It made for a joyful experience as local residents, starved of their usual modern means of entertainment, took to the streets and talked to each other.

For a few hours Stratford returned to the 'old days'. Many citizens found their way to an outdoor concert that was being held in a bandstand on Veteran's Drive. Complete with a barbecue, it was a fun event in which numerous local musicians performed acoustically, with no electric guitars in sight! All sorts of acts took part, with musical styles ranging from rock 'n' roll to bluegrass. To loud applause from the audience, Justin performed a duet with his mother Pattie, and was described by one report as 'a fan favourite'. He had clearly turned his Stratford Star experience to his advantage.

The competition had another hugely important influence on Justin: he realized that singing and performing was what he wanted to do with his life. 'That's when I figured out I really wanted to sing, it was my passion,' Justin said of his participation in the contest. It has been reported that Justin finished second in the September 2007 competition, but one of the organizers says that there was a misunderstanding. According to Angie Adair, who helped count the votes, only the winner was announced on the night. Justin actually finished third, she said, coming behind the two older girls.

Either way, Justin had done very well in a contest dominated by singers older than him. Mimi Price, another of the contest organizers, noticed straightaway that Justin was no ordinary child. 'We knew there was something special, but we thought, "Give him a couple years with voice training and he would have the whole package,"' she told *The Toronto Star*. 'He was definitely up for the challenge and he had the charisma, he just didn't have the experience.' Nowadays, looking at the Justin Bieber who performs as a professional singer, she is impressed, particularly with his dancing ability. 'His moves, my goodness!' she said.

My goodness indeed! Little could Price or anyone else have known at the time that the videos of Justin's performances that his mother had filmed on her handheld camera would be the springboard for him to become a global superstar. Pattie had originally filmed her son to keep a record for herself, and to share with family members and friends who had wanted to be at the contest but were unable to attend. Pattie had been there and so had Justin's grandparents but others missed out, including his father.

Both Pattie and Justin were proud of what he had achieved, so when they went home after the contest ended they were keen to share the videos of his songs with the relatives and friends who had missed out. They considered putting the videos onto disks that they could post out, or even emailing them as attachments around interested people. Both of these routes had complications though, and they decided that there must be a simpler way . . .

The answer came to them suddenly: the video-sharing website YouTube was the perfect way for them to share Pattie's videos! All they had to do was upload the videos onto the website and then email links to anyone interested in watching them.

Justin opened his own YouTube account under the username 'kidrauhl'. He has never explained why he chose this username. Some people think it might mean 'Kid Rule', others believe he chose it because his father had a similar username for his own online activities. Either way, the name would soon become globally known – because his YouTube account was destined to be a huge success.

'I put my singing videos from the competition on YouTube so that my friends and family could watch them,' Justin remembered. 'But it turned out that other people liked them,' he added, in something of an understatement. Before long, his YouTube account had become a big hit and was soon an Internet sensation.

The realization that his videos were being watched by more than just his family and friends dawned slowly on young Justin. 'I was like, well, I don't have a 100 people in my family,' he said, remembering how the hit tally rose. 'And then I was like, I don't have 500 people in my family. And it just kept getting bigger and bigger.'

Although Justin has at times spoken as if his pop career was not a long-held dream of his, he has also said that he had wanted to do something musical with his life for as long as he could remember. 'I always really wanted to be a musician, but I didn't really know what I wanted to do,' he told *MTV News*. 'I was just doing it for fun, basically.' His journey might have been unplanned, but he was edging ever closer to the ultimate destination. The next stage of Justin's amazing ascent to the top was under way . . .

3

A Champion Channel

ustin's videos were perfect for YouTube. He was cute and talented, as anyone watching them could see. The home-made style of the videos he continued to upload made them all the more attractive and enjoyable. People were charmed by this kid, who seemed not just talented but genuine and down-to-earth. The YouTube site allows users to 'rate' videos they watch and also provide feedback. As the 'hit counter' for his videos shot upwards, Justin began to receive a deluge of positive feedback from people who had watched and loved them. He was building quite an online fanbase. Their comments varied but they were nearly all admiring and most agreed on one thing: they wanted to see more videos from Justin!

Over the next few months he performed more songs as his mother filmed him and they uploaded the best of them onto the YouTube channel. After his Stratford Star videos had proved so popular he began to upload videos filmed at his home. The first featured him playing on the keyboard a song written by his grandmother. He is seen wearing a light blue T-shirt pulled over a dark blue jumper. There are two guitars in the background, underlining what a musical household he lived in.

Pattie's caption for the video acknowledges that he might not be playing the tune completely perfectly, 'but I think it's close'. Mostly shot from Justin's side, during the video he looks over his shoulder into the camera a few times. The tune he is playing is gentle and almost hypnotizes the listener. Uploaded in January 2007, this video has now been watched on YouTube well over a million times.

The website that hosted Justin's videos with such remarkable success was launched two years before he created his own channel. Founded by three men – Chad Hurley, Jawed Karim and Steve Chen – their inspiration in launching YouTube mirrors the reason Justin first used it. Chen, so the official story goes, had thrown a party and wanted to find an easy way of sharing a video of the evening with his friends. So, based in an office above a pizzeria and a Japanese restaurant, they got to work, first launching the site with a video of Karim's visit to a zoo.

Within a year of the website's launch the site had more than 65,000 new videos uploaded daily – and 100 million video views. It has since been bought by the giant Internet company Google and struck deals with movie giants like MGM and Lionsgate, as well as television companies such as CBS. YouTube now receives over 2 million views each day. It features all manner of videos, including some amusing ones such as *Scarlet Takes a Tumble*. This video features a girl singing to the camera. She stands on a coffee table for extra performance and all seems well . . . until she slips off the table and lands crashing on the floor. This is the video Justin says is his favourite on the YouTube website. It is so popular that people have added videos to YouTube showing their reaction to it.

However, at this stage Justin was not only watching YouTube videos but starring in them! Four days later Pattie and Justin added another video to his channel, in which he plays guitar and sings 'Refine Me' by Jennifer Knapp. For this one he is sitting on the sofa in their living room and the lamp next to him is switched on, suggesting it was filmed in the evening. He is wearing a grey jumper with the hood pulled over his head. He strums the guitar left-handed and sings the song's soulful, religious lyrics with his characteristic mixture of sweetness and power. Only one verse and chorus are recorded, but Justin delivers them so well that the shortness of the video doesn't matter. Indeed, it left the viewers wanting more – which is always a good thing to do as you build an Internet following.

It was to be over two months before the next video was added to the channel, but even during the break in uploads people continued to watch his existing videos and praise them highly.

On 25 April 2007 the next video was added to the channel. In the accompanying text, Pattie wrote: 'I caught him just

before he was brushing his teeth,' as he sang the song 'Back at One' by the R&B musician Brian McKnight. So Pattie asked him to carrying on singing while she filmed. 'He's just messing around here but I think [it's] cute and funny,' she wrote, adding that 'his hair has grown back now'.

The last statement refers to the eye-catching hairstyle Justin has in the video. His hair has been cropped short and tramlines had been cut into it all over. What matters most, though, is how well he sings, even as he is preparing to brush his teeth. The video begins with him singing the chorus and right away it is clear that Justin, who had shown on previous videos that he has a great voice for pop and folk songs, can also sing with a more edgy, R&B style. As he gets to the line that addresses the female subject of the song, he turns and looks into the camera.

The whole performance is very polished. Anyone who has since watched his official promotional video for his song 'One Time' will notice there are a few similarities here. For a start, when he sings the word 'one' he holds up one finger, just as he does on the 'One Time' video. Likewise, he holds his palm flat against his chest occasionally, a movement he has used regularly during performances since becoming famous. However, back then his videos were more rough-and-ready – which was part of their charm.

At the end of the 'Back at One' video Justin forgets the words and merely hums the tune before cheekily incorporating: 'Forget the words . . . brush my teeth' into the tune. The video ends with him grabbing the toothpaste tube ready to do just that. At the time of writing, the video has been viewed nearly 5 million times. Later that same day, another video was added to the channel. Here he is filmed standing against a plain wall singing 'snippets' of 'Because of You' by Ne-Yo. Pattie makes sure that she films Justin from above for part of the song, so his 'tramlines' hairstyle can be clearly seen. Justin swings his torso from side to side as he sings and appears to be almost in ecstasy as he sings the soulful lyrics.

The videos were proving ever more popular as Justin showed different elements of his musical range and personality with each new one uploaded. The contrasts were made clear by the fact that, following two successive R&B-style songs, the next one that Justin and Pattie uploaded was a piece by indie rock singer Edwin McCain. The song Justin chose to cover was 'I'll Be', which was a hit for McCain in 1998 (when Justin was only four years old!). For this video Justin seems to have filmed it himself, simply by placing the camera flat on the table in front of the living-room sofa. At the end, the viewer can see Justin reaching over to switch the camera off.

At two minutes and ten seconds, this one is longer than some of his previous videos and he sings the song brilliantly. He also strums his guitar well, a fact that is sometimes overlooked due to the strength of his voice. Interestingly,

Justin twice skips the line about 'love's suicide'. The other stand-out fact about this video is that it is filmed in a 'sepia' tone, which gives it a warmer, slightly more professional look than his previous efforts.

The fan base for the 'kidrauhl' channel was growing and growing. Justin and Pattie realized he had a major audience and that among the thousands of people who were watching each video there might be important contacts from the entertainment industry. They decided to showcase the full range of his talents on the channel. He had so far been featured singing, playing guitar and keyboard.

The next two videos – uploaded in July and August of 2007 – were to show off how great he was on the drums. The first one was a forty-second video of Justin dressed in a simple T-shirt and shorts, sitting on the sofa playing an African drum called a *djembe*. The *djembe* has become a popular instrument among rock musicians and has been used by everyone from The Beatles to U2. Justin plays it well and, although short, the video shows the world that this boy has many musical talents.

The second video, added in August, is over two minutes long and sees Justin wearing a white-and-black hooded jumper and a black cap. He is filmed onstage prior to an unspecified outdoor concert, playing a white drum kit. This is the first live concert that Justin is widely known to have taken part in, and in it he shows that being small in size does not mean you can't hit the drums hard and well. That same day a video from the actual show itself was added, and the fact that the concert was outdoors is clear from the sound of the wind blowing around him. This video features Justin performing the Lifehouse song 'You and Me'. He is sitting on the stage, playing his guitar as he sings. This love song was released two years before the video was shot, and Justin's great rendition of it goes down well with the audience at the concert. They whoop and cheer at the end, prompting a shy and sweet 'Thank you' from Justin in return. What is most impressive about this video is how at ease Justin is on the stage.

No wonder the positive feedback was flowing his way from YouTube browsers. Word was spreading like wildfire about the amazing Canadian kid with the wonderful voice and great musical talent. 'People were watching it and people were subscribing,' he remembered. As well as praise, Justin was also starting to receive requests for further songs chosen by his growing Internet fan base. Other fans asked questions or just made excited comments.

Interestingly, while Justin was sharing his videos for anyone to see on YouTube, he also kept quiet about what he was doing among his classmates and friends. 'I didn't tell my friends because they didn't really know that I could sing,' he said. 'They knew me for playing sports. I just wanted to be a regular kid, and I knew they wouldn't treat me the same way if I told them.'

Justin has always been a humble character and he has held on to this great characteristic throughout his rise to the top. So it's no surprise that he was not showing off at school about his popularity on the World Wide Web. It might have proved a great answer to the playground bullies, or it might have made it worse to show them how popular he was proving in the wider world.

That popularity was growing all the time. People were fascinated by Justin and the Internet hit rate was rising, as was the level of positive feedback he was getting. Among those who contacted him via his YouTube channel were some representatives from a Toronto-based company called Rapid Discovery Media (RDM). The company – which specializes in helping promote people via the Internet – was just two years old when Justin came to its attention. As its MySpace profile boasts: 'Whether unsigned and unheard or a top subscribed celebrity, our experts are here to help with your production, promotion and financial goals.'

The people at RDM were amazed by Justin's talent and they felt that they could help make his already thriving YouTube channel even more popular. They had little doubt that Justin had all the makings of a pop sensation and felt that – in keeping with their company's name – they could help him achieve that more quickly. Pattie and Justin were both ambitious for him, but they were also cautious and thought over the offer and its implications before deciding how to respond. In the end, they decided that Rapid Discovery Media seemed like good, experienced and bright people and decided to work with them. It was not a decision they would regret.

The company were true to their name, and did indeed act 'rapidly' on Justin's behalf. They redesigned his YouTube channel, offered him technical know-how to improve the quality and appeal of his videos and also helped him open an account on the popular social-networking website MySpace. They also simultaneously began to host his videos on their own YouTube channel as well, which helped bring them to ever more new fans.

Justin had been doing very well building a following on his own, but with the experts on his side throwing all their knowledge and enthusiasm behind his quest, he was soon on a roll. While they were helping him build his fan club, RDM were also insistent that Justin himself carried on doing what he already did best – recording fantastic music videos for his YouTube channel. There would soon be even more new attention-grabbing videos there. Justin was moving ever closer to his first big break in the record industry itself.

It is worth remembering that as all this was going on, Justin was just a normal teenage boy, doing what teenage boys do. As we have seen, he kept quiet at school about his online exploits. He continued to play sports, including football and hockey. He went to school and to church. Here was a playful and cheeky kid who did not change at all, even as his YouTube channel began to turn him into an Internet celebrity.

As Rapid Discovery Media busily worked to fine-tune and promote his talents to even wider audiences, Justin kept his feet on the ground and went on doing the thing that he is better at than anyone else on the planet – being Justin Bieber!

As more people noticed his singing talent on his YouTube channel, Justin began to receive requests from some viewers. One of the songs that people asked him to sing was 'Do You?' by Ne-Yo. He had already shown he could perform a Ne-Yo song well. With this new challenge set by his fans he was able to reaffirm his range and talent once again.

He uploaded the video in September 2007 and it instantly drew glowing comments and ratings from his viewers. He was filmed wearing a white T-shirt and standing against a plain black background and, although the video was not lit properly, it had a more professional feel than some of his previous efforts. As he sang the line about wondering whether 'you ever think of me any more', there was an element of irony in it. Justin's fans *were* thinking of him – all the time – and waiting for him to add more songs to his website.

They did not have to wait long because later the same day he uploaded his cover of 'Wait for You' by Elliott Yamin. Yamin is an American singer who came to fame as a result of the reality-television show *American Idol*. He came third in the fifth series of the show but managed to carve out a successful career for himself despite not winning.

Chosen as a result of another request from browsers, 'Wait for You' is a slow, moving ballad and Justin sings it very well on the video. His characteristic habit of placing his palm against his chest during particularly emotional lines is on show again. This was shot inside his home and was the last video to be located there for a while: the next few videos would be set elsewhere, as Justin ensured he maintained variety on his channel.

In October 2007 Justin uploaded a video of him playing live onstage with a rock band. Justin is on drums in the band known only as The Amazing Kids. The guitarists are called JD and Alex Tintinalli, while the bassist is unnamed, and they are playing the legendary rock song 'Free Bird'. First released by Lynyrd Skynyrd in the 1970s, 'Free Bird' has since become a hugely popular song, which can be very long – lasting up to fifteen minutes when played live, with many of those minutes taken up by instrumental jamming.

When The Amazing Kids played it live they were clearly following this lead and Justin takes them through their paces, setting a fine and consistent beat on his black drum kit. The section of their performance featured on YouTube is split over two separate videos. As the caption for the second video promises: 'Justin Bieber goes wild on drums in this clip.' It does not disappoint. As is customary for the drummer in the song he hits the drums hard, with some fantastic rolls, one of which brings the song to a crashing conclusion. It is one of those songs in which the drummer, normally upstaged by the theatrics of other members of the band, becomes the focus of attention.

At the end, the audience cheers its appreciation and one of his bandmates immediately singles Justin out for a special reception. 'Justin on drums, give it up!' says the bandmate and the audience responds ecstatically.

By moving the location for this video from the sitting room to the stage, Justin had shown just how ready he was for a professional career. Since he could play the drums so well on a grown-up, energetic rock song as well as singing sweet ballads and edgy R&B tunes, he was truly a multi-talented boy.

When he recorded his next song for YouTube, Justin could never have realized that within a couple of years he would sing the same song again, though this time not for an Internet audience but for a very prestigious audience in an incredible setting. The song was 'Someday at Christmas', which had been recorded by soul legend Stevie Wonder in the 1960s, and its idealistic and hopeful messages have led to it being compared with 'Imagine' by John Lennon.

A very powerful song, Justin's live performance of it is amazing, by far his best to date. He performs it with his characteristic combination of youthful sweetness and a maturity beyond his years. As he sings the idealistic lyrics about a world without war or poverty, the listener manages to believe, for a couple of minutes, that such things are possible.

The video was first uploaded in rough form in November 2007 but a higher-quality version was added the following month, on Christmas Eve. Justin sang so well that even reality-television judge Simon Cowell would have been unable to find fault with his performance. At the time Justin could never have guessed that he would be singing the song again, but this time to the President of the United States of America!

In between these two uploads Justin had added footage of him singing a moving ballad called 'Set a Place at Your Table'. He is shown recording the song for a Christmas CD that was sold locally to raise money for a food bank. The song is appropriate for the charity setting because it is about laying a place at the table for someone in need and drawing hope from the experience. With a choir backing him on the vocals, Justin has rarely sounded sweeter and more soulful.

'Very nice,' comes a producer's voice at the end. 'Thank yooooouuu,' replies Justin. As the video ends, a message flashes up on the screen: 'Merry Christmas from Justin Bieber'.

It had been an amazing year for him. As a result of his YouTube exploits, Justin ended the year with thousands of fans who had never heard of him the previous Christmas. A merry Christmas indeed for him and Pattie. They could not know what 2008 would bring, but must have suspected – at least a little – that great things were on the horizon.

The first video of the new year was added by Justin in February. In it he sang the Chris Brown song 'With You', and it is with this video that the influence of Rapid Discovery Media is first really noticed. He is wearing a cool jumper with graffiti-like writing on it.

He begins the song sitting on a sofa but gets up midway through and stands for the rest of the performance. There are posters on his wall including one of the cartoon series *The Simpsons* and one of the rap artist Tupac Shakur. Justin sings the song to an instrumental backing track, and the video is better lit than some of his previous efforts. The way he dances and uses his hands to express the lyrics makes this performance similar to the one he was to give later in the 'One Time' video.

Again, the video was quickly gaining excited and glowing feedback on the Web, but a few days after it went live Justin received praise for his performance from an unexpected source: Chris Brown, the man who originally sang 'With You', was the unexpected caller. He was impressed by Justin's cover version of the song and congratulated him on the performance. 'I talked to him on the phone and stuff,' confirmed Justin.

With praise now coming from famous professional singers, Justin's confidence was really soaring. Maybe he really was cut out for a career as a famous pop artist. All of the praise he was getting filled him with hope and determination. He had a fan base by now and felt he had to keep going with the music just to keep them happy. Fortunately, continuing with his music made him happy too – so everyone was a winner as Justin went on building his YouTube page!

Later in the same month, Justin had his guitar out again as he covered 'Cry Me a River'. He was wearing a cute cap and sitting on the living-room sofa as he sang the atmospheric song which had been such a huge hit for his namesake Justin Timberlake in December 2002. It also won young Mr Timberlake a Grammy Award for Best Male Pop Vocal Performance two years later. As his online fans had come to expect of our Justin, he handled the song perfectly both in the guitar-playing and his singing, which was just as mournful and soulful as the song demanded.

Justin had been blown away by the call from Chris Brown in the wake of his 'With You' cover, but he could never have believed at the time that he would soon be the subject of a tug-of-war between Timberlake and another hot star, with both men desperate to sign a management deal with him. In the caption for the video an explanation of how to pronounce Justin's surname was added: 'it sounds like Beeber'. With news of his talent spreading so quickly by word of mouth, Justin and his team were keen to ensure that his name was pronounced correctly!

One of the many artists with whom Justin Timberlake had duetted is Dutch singer Esmée Denters. She is also signed to his record label. On 2 March 2008 a video was added to the 'kidrauhl' YouTube channel of Justin Bieber singing 'With You' again. However, this was a very different video from his first cover of the song. Wearing a blue cap, blue T-shirt and red sporty shorts, Justin is seen in a new location to his previous videos, standing in a brightly painted room with a painting of a guitar hanging on the yellow walls.

Sitting on the sofa in front of him is Esmée Denters, and it is to her that he sings the song. Justin seems very relaxed as he playfully flirts with her during the song – and even the moments when he seems a little uncomfortable only add to the cuteness of the video.

Denters is six years older than Justin but she seems to find his performance fun and impressive. At the end she high-fives Justin and says: 'Wow! That was awesome! Very talented!'

It was testament to how far his YouTube channel had come in little over a year. It started with a handful of roughly filmed videos of him performing at the Stratford Star competition, uploaded purely for family and close friends to enjoy. Then some were added of Justin singing and playing instruments in his home. As the popularity built he had begun to vary the nature of the videos: a few of him performing live on stage with either guitar or drums; some of him playing just keyboards or drums with no accompaniments. Now he was shown playfully singing a romantic song to a well-known recording artist.

RDM proudly claims a large slice of credit for Justin's success in building his popularity through YouTube. The company's website proudly boasts: 'RDM was responsible for boosting Justin's YouTube presence to the top 100 subscribed channels of all time, and #1 musician in his country on YouTube, expanding his reach from 100 to 100,000 subscribers, as well as creating and managing his MySpace channel, ranking in the top 10 musicians of his country, and #1 in his genre with over 50,000 friends in his first 10 months.'

He was proving to be a shining example of how musicians can be promoted through the Internet. But Justin is not the only music artist to use the Internet so brilliantly. British pop singer Lily Allen had been rejected by several record labels and had almost given up on her dream of becoming a pop star before she changed her mind and decided to give it one more go. She posted 'demo' versions of her songs onto her MySpace profile to test the public reaction, and she soon picked up a fanatical online following. As she picked up tens of thousands of MySpace fans, Lily's unconventional way of promoting her music meant the media wrote about her, which led to her picking up even more fans. She has since become a pop sensation, selling millions of albums and winning important awards including a Mercury Prize and an Ivor Novello.

A very similar technique was used by British indie band Arctic Monkeys, who are best known for their catchy single 'I Bet You Look Good on the Dancefloor', which was a Number 1 hit in the UK. Their fame grew via MySpace, though there is a dispute over whether this was a deliberate tactic from them or whether it was their fans that drove their Internet fame.

The American singer Savannah Outen also used the Internet to launch her career, though she chose to take the same route as Justin – posting videos of her singing on

YouTube. The first video she posted was of the song 'Listen' from the movie *Dreamgirls*. It received a great deal of online praise and requests for her to record more videos, and she is now an established recording artist who is particularly popular among the Disney audience. She has landed many endorsement deals, and her YouTube videos have been viewed nearly 50 million times.

Much the same route launched the career of Portuguese singer Mia Rose. Then a student, Mia began posting songs on the site during her Christmas holidays in 2006. Before long she was the most subscribed-to performer on YouTube and has since launched a successful career with a record label and a lot of media coverage.

Similarly, Esmée Denters, the Dutch star to whom Justin sang on one of his YouTube videos, was also signed by a label as a result of her online video postings. She also kicked off her online campaign in 2006 and after coming to the attention of a leading music manager she was signed by Tennman Records, the label run by pop star Justin Timberlake.

As we'll see, there are some other parallels between Justin Bieber's career and that of Denters. Other acts to successfully use the Internet to build their fame include Scottish singer-songwriter Sandi Thorn, who used 'webcasts' to great effect in 2006. She now has a record deal with the RCA label.

Sometimes artists have used YouTube promotion at the same time as following a more mainstream route to fame. There is no better example of this than reality show superstar Susan Boyle. The unknown Scottish singer gave a memorable audition to the third series of *Britain's Got Talent*. When she appeared on the stage and said she wanted to be a successful singer, most of the audience – and judges – rolled their eyes in disbelief. She didn't look like a star and they doubted that she would sound like one either. Everybody was expecting another hilarious television moment of an auditionee who thought they were great but were actually terrible.

Then she began to sing 'I Dreamed a Dream', and it transpired that she was a magnificent singer. The audience turned in her favour and, by the end of the song, she had the entire theatre on their feet roaring their appreciation. She was through to the next round for sure, but before then she became an instant worldwide sensation after a YouTube video of the audition was watched by millions of Internet-users across the globe. Boyle quickly became one of the most famous people on earth – and she had only done one audition on a British show! She is now smashing CD sales records around the world and has sold millions of copies of her debut album.

As for Justin, he says he never dreamed a dream and was instead taken by surprise. 'I never dreamed that posting videos online would change my life,' he said. But as his YouTube following soared higher and higher he wondered what he could do next to make his music even more well known.

He had earned himself a following by uploading his songs onto YouTube. Since RDM had become involved his popularity had increased. And it was not just 'ordinary' people who were watching his videos: as the phone call from Chris Brown has shown, people in the record industry were beginning to sit up and take notice of the cute kid from Canada. In just seven months his videos had been watched 10 million times!

One day a man from America stumbled upon Justin's YouTube channel. He clicked on a few of Justin's videos and really liked what he saw and heard. So much so that neither his, nor Justin's, life would ever be the same again. Although he didn't know it immediately, Justin had just got the break that would take him to the very top of the tree.

And it was all going to happen very, very quickly – again, taking Justin by surprise. 'Being famous was never in my mind,' he has said. 'Also, like, Stratford, Ontario . . . a little town of 30,000 in the middle of nowhere? It was something I didn't think was possible. I owe everything to my fans and YouTube.' He has always been keen to credit those who have helped him get along in life. Well, there would soon be all the more reason for him to issue this sort of credit.

Hold on tight, for Justin's story is about to enter true rollercoaster territory . . .

4

Ushered In

Most people know the story of Cinderella. It's a popular fairy tale that has been told for generations through books, plays and films, the story of a girl who rises above difficult circumstances to go to the royal ball at the palace. There are similarities between Justin's story and that of Cinderella, as a key person in his life has pointed out. Justin has also sung of Cinderella in one of his hit songs. In his case, there are plenty of candidates who could be considered the 'fairy godmother' who helped him 'go to the ball', although most of them are male! Justin was fortunate, though, that his talent and his loveable personality meant he made friends and won admirers wherever he turned. He would soon be going to the ball.

As Justin's YouTube videos began to be watched by more and more fans, they also attracted the attention of a growing number of talent scouts, who are always prowling in hope of discovering the 'next big thing'. Some of these people are serious and genuine professionals with the contacts and know-how to turn promising performers into stars. Others, though, are less reputable characters who should not be taken seriously by young hopefuls and their loved ones.

Pattie shared and encouraged Justin's dream of taking his singing to the next level, but both of them were also sensibly cautious in their ambitions. Justin's upbringing might have been short on luxuries, but it was high on wholesome love. He is therefore a boy with his head screwed on and not one who was about to take a leap into the unknown at the drop of a hat. The first flurry of offers to come his way from would-be managers were, therefore, politely declined. Some of those who approached were very persistent, but to no avail. Like many people with genuine talent, Justin was being encouraged by those nearest to him to believe that one day the right opportunity would arise – and that until then it was correct to wait.

'I was contacted by many different record executives, a lot of different managers and agents,' Justin told the Canadian magazine *Maclean's*. He did not jump at the first chance, though. 'My mom was basically like, "Justin, I don't think this is going to happen, it's not going to work. We don't have a lawyer, we don't have money for a lawyer, and we're not going to just sign something that we don't know what it says." So we ended up just declining all these people.'

Meanwhile, as Justin waited as patiently as he could, his mother was actually busily at work on his behalf. Pattie reportedly contacted an entertainment lawyer in Los Angeles to ask for advice on how best to take things forward for her son. Soon after this, she was contacted by a remarkable young man who would change Justin's life forever.

This man had watched some of Justin's YouTube videos and been stunned by what he saw and heard. He was particularly impressed by the video of Justin's cover of the Ne-Yo song 'So Sick', the one in which he sported those memorable tramlines in his hair.

'I was blown away that a little kid had a range like that,' he remembered from the fateful evening he first watched it. 'Then I stalked him,' he added, jokingly. However, despite the joke, this man was actually *very* serious about Justin and his career potential. Given his own track record in business, this man's approval was not something to be taken lightly. So who was this man? And how did he go about convincing an initially reluctant Pattie to allow Justin to sign with him so he could first fulfil – and then exceed – their wildest dreams?

Step forward, Scott Braun – better known nowadays as Scooter Braun. Born in Greenwich, Connecticut in 1982, a full twelve years before Justin was even born, Scooter Braun has long been a very enterprising man. At school he was a successful, popular pupil and was voted in as the high school president. While he was still in his first year at Emory University in Atlanta, he started his first-ever business.

In a way Scooter Braun was like Justin – he wanted to earn his own money so he was not reliant on his parents for handouts; just as Justin busked to try and gain some independence, so did Braun start his own business. Also, like Justin, when Braun spotted the right opportunity, he grabbed it with both hands. For example, while at university he noted that an Atlanta nightclub called Paradox was struggling to get any customers through its door on Thursday evenings. So he arranged a Thursday evening party there on the understanding that while the club took all the profits from drinks, he would get all the profits from the entry fees. Come the day, over 1,000 people arrived – and Braun was in the money as a result. He went on to arrange further Thursday evening parties and was soon building himself quite a reputation as a party organizer.

Before long, the well-known rapper Ludacris contacted Braun, who he had met at a club, and asked him to organize parties for him as he toured around America alongside Eminem. Braun took the challenge on and arranged successful bashes in New York, Miami, Atlanta, Tampa and Hartford. Not even out of his teens yet, Braun was shaping up to be quite the successful businessman.

He left university early, which initially dismayed his father, but he went on to justify his decision. His reputation spread and he went on to arrange social events for other famous people and also began networking in the music world.

Then one day he got a phone call from a music producer

called Jermaine Dupri. Having produced hit albums for Mariah Carey and Usher, Dupri was a respected and successful figure in the music industry. Highly impressed with Braun's track record, Dupri hired him to his record label, So So Def Records. Based in Atlanta, Georgia, it specializes in hip-hop and soul music.

Braun soared within the organization and quickly attained the impressive job title of Executive Director of Marketing. Among his fellow workers he had a less formal but equally positive title: 'Hustla', a streetwise spelling of the word 'hustler'. Braun was delighted to be called this, as to him, 'a hustla is somebody that doesn't take no for an answer; somebody who had a vision and a goal and works to realize it; somebody who works his [butt] off to make it happen'.

Long before he crossed paths with Justin, Braun was a man on the go, driving a flash purple Mercedes CLK 320 and arranging parties involving A-list celebrities, including the likes of Britney Spears and rubbing shoulders with hip-hop royalty including Kanye West.

Braun certainly had plenty of vision and was a ferociously hard worker. In 2004, at the age of twenty-three, he took the brave step of leaving So So Def because he wanted to form his own company, which he called SB Projects. It is an entertainment and promotion company with a wide range of projects and ambitions. This is entirely in keeping with the man himself, who has always had multiple things on the go at once, so much so that a friend of his once admitted he couldn't even quite keep up with Braun's ventures.

SB Projects touched on the film, television and music

industries to name but three. Its client list is hugely varied and includes musicians, car companies and American Football teams among many, many others. So successful has Braun become in so many different fields that the influential American magazine *Billboard* once named him in a poll of the leading 'power players' of the year.

Something that everybody who has dealt with Braun would surely agree on is that he deserves every bit of his success. However he was about to take an already highly successful career to dizzying new heights – and Justin would be the vehicle for that trip.

Soon after he formed his own company, Braun took some time off to go and watch a basketball game. As ever with Braun, even when safely away from the office he found it hard to entirely switch off from work. He lives for success and his head is always buzzing with ideas and dreams. As he was chatting at the game with Ludacris's manager, Chaka Zulu, Braun outlined his ambitions for the immediate future.

The first was to launch the next big white rap artist. He also explained that he wanted to sign a girl band and a boy singer who 'could do it like Michael Jackson – sing songs that adults would appreciate and be reminded of the innocence they once felt about love'. These might have sounded like big dreams, but Braun is one of those people who often gets what he hopes for. It's not a question of luck so much as one of determination, energy and imagination.

He discovered his white rapper within weeks, when he signed MC Asher Roth, who quickly had a hit with 'I Love College'. Roth's debut album was a Top 5 hit in America. As for Braun's 'next Michael Jackson' hope, that huge ambition was met while he was browsing the Internet one evening. Expanding on what he was looking for, Braun said: 'I wanted someone who was like Michael. Someone who captivated not only kids, but adults, too.' As he stumbled upon his first video of Justin singing, Braun thought he had found that. Indeed, he was so excited he thought he had struck gold.

It was, so the story goes, quite by chance that Braun first came across Justin's online presence. 'I was consulting for an act that Akon had in a production deal and I was looking at his YouTube videos,' Braun has said. He continues, explaining that it was the 'Related Videos' function of YouTube that led him to Justin.

'The kid was singing Aretha Franklin's "Respect", and there was a related video of Justin singing the same song. I clicked on it, thinking it was the same kid, and realized that the twenty-year-old I was watching was now twelve.' His reaction on watching Justin's performance of 'Respect' – taken from the Stratford Star competition – was one of enormous excitement. Not just emotionally, but physically too! 'It was such raw talent, my gut just went wild,' Braun said. Ever the joker, he added: 'Maybe I shouldn't tell people I watched videos of Justin Bieber in the middle of the night.'

On a more serious note, Braun really was amazed by Justin's ability. The more of Justin's YouTube videos he clicked through, the higher his admiration rose.

'I was really impressed with, you know, how young he was and how he was holding the crowd with his guitar and, you know, he was raw talent,' Braun later told a television show. Could this be the boy to fill his 'Michael Jackson' ambition? Braun was in no doubt at all. He recalled: 'I said, "I need to find this kid."'

But finding him was going to be a little easier said than done. Even once he did track Justin's family down, it was not going to be a straightforward process to convince them to sign up with him. Pattie is a loving and responsible mother who was keen for Justin to excel in life but also keen to protect him as best she could. She had already turned away some offers to manage her son – and she was not about to easily give up the protective arm she wrapped round him.

'My mom was like, "Who is this guy?",' remembered Justin. 'And then she went and called him to get rid of him.' However, among the things Braun has never lacked are ambition, determination and charm. Which was just as well, as he would need plenty of each to get his way.

So, how had he first gone about contacting Justin Bieber, the kid from YouTube? Braun was rightly concerned that an approach from an adult to a schoolboy might easily be perceived as inappropriate and sinister. If he did not handle the approach sensibly he would be in danger of blowing it from the off. So as he homed in on Justin he took steps to make sure that it was as clear as possible that he had nothing but honest intentions.

'I got in touch with the school board of three different areas from the Google banners, and told them I'm looking for this kid, and please have his mother call me from an unknown number, so she doesn't feel like I'm a weirdo,' Braun remembered. However, it was never going to be as simple as that, and he needed to leave many messages in many different places before he stood a chance of hearing back.

Pattie had hoped that Justin might become a singer in a Christian style, so she wondered why someone of a different faith had been sent to help him. 'I prayed, "God, you don't want this Jewish kid to be Justin's man, do you?"' she recalled. She was also concerned that this 'kid with a Gmail address didn't sound very professional'. Clearly, Braun had some convincing to do.

Although Justin and his mother initially rebuffed the offer to communicate with Braun, they soon realized that he was extremely keen to talk with them. 'He was very, very persistent,' Justin revealed to *Billboard* as he looked back over Braun's tactics. 'He even called my great aunt and my school board.'

Here, Braun's tactics are similar to the ones used by reality television giant Simon Cowell many years ago when he wanted to sign two actors he had seen on a television series called *Soldier, Soldier*. When persistent calls to the two actors themselves did not convince them to sign a record deal with him, Cowell began contacting their relatives in the hope of convincing them that way. He was convinced he could make a hit record with them and was also sure that as long as he kept piling on the pressure, they would eventually see his point of view. The people who do best in the entertainment industry often seem to be those who have both the vision to see an opportunity where others do not and the persistence to make that opportunity come true. It has worked wonders for Simon Cowell – and it was about to work very neatly for Scooter Braun.

Finally, Braun got hold of Pattie and they spoke for over two hours on the phone. As we have seen, initially Pattie had phoned him with every intention of telling him to leave them alone once and for all: this was to be the last she would hear from this Scooter Braun, she believed. But never underestimate his powers of persuasion! With his persistence having taken him this far, it was now time for Braun to draw on his reserves of charm.

He explained his wonderment at Justin's talent and potential. He explained how much he loves music and how well he understands the record industry. Justin, he assured Pattie, had a very bright future ahead of him. He also convinced her that he was the one to guide Justin to it. As the conversation wore on, Braun relaxed and let it move into different areas. It was important to build up a general rapport with Pattie, he realized. Asked later what the conversation was about, Braun put it very simply: 'We talked about life'. His way with words was clearly a winning one on the day, and as a result of the call Pattie agreed that she and Justin would discuss the offer Braun had put to her.

'My mom had that gut feeling,' said Justin. 'I think moms generally know when they have their gut feelings.' Once mother and son had talked it over, they agreed to meet

How it all began:
Justin with his mentor
and friend Usher (left);
and at the launch
of his debut album
(below).

Justin performs at the Nintendo World Store in New York.

Unstoppable: not even a foot fracture holds Justin back as he rocks the Jingle Ball in December 2009 (right and overleaf).

Facing page: Justin Bieber – heart-throb.

Justin's world: 'Bieber Fever' hits the UK as Justin signs copies of his album *My World* in London, England.

Favourite girl: Justin attends the 2010 Grammy Awards with his mother, Pattie Mallette …

… and rubs shoulders with fellow musical greats, such as Fergie from the Black Eyed Peas.

Help Haiti: in the wake of the earthquake in Haiti, Justin was keen to contribute to the humanitarian response, recording a section for the US charity single (right) and performing at a fund-raising concert (below), at which he met former US President Bill Clinton (below right).

Overleaf: Justin at his sell-out concert at the Hollywood Palladium.

Braun. 'And it turned out he was a cool guy,' Justin told the *Toronto Star.*

Justin was on the up – quite literally, as he flew to America to meet Braun and spend time at a recording studio. It was a no-strings meeting arranged by Braun, and the idea was that Justin and Pattie would get the chance to meet him face to face and decide what they wanted to do next. 'He flew me out to Atlanta,' said Justin. 'I got to meet him, great guy, really solid guy. Ended up hanging out with him.'

It has been suggested that when Justin and Pattie flew to Atlanta to meet Braun this was their first time on an aeroplane. However, it is unlikely that their trip for the holiday in Florida would have been made by any other mode of transport. Whatever the case, flying to America for a meeting with an influential music man was certainly a brand new experience for Justin.

He was excited but also a bit nervous as the plane took off from Canada. Both feelings grew as it landed again in America, the land of opportunity and dreams. He and Pattie were rushed off to meet Braun. It was the dawn of a great relationship.

As Justin was 'hanging out' with Braun, they quickly built up a great understanding. Although Braun is twelve years older than Justin they share some key characteristics.

Both began to excel in their chosen fields from a young age; both are quick to spot opportunities that are open to them. Braun grew up in a more privileged family than Justin's, but he still shares the hunger for success that first drove Justin to busk and then to build his YouTube channel into the successful tool it was. Therefore they hit it off well and it was soon clear to both that they wanted to work together.

Braun was taken not just by Justin's musical talent, but also by his loveable and sometimes cheeky personality. Justin tends to light up rooms as he enters them and wins fans quickly. Not only could Braun see that this would be a great asset for Justin's career, it would also make him a fun and rewarding person to work with.

What happened next was, according to the Justin Bieber legend, a strange coincidence. As Justin and Braun arrived in the studio car park, they happened to spot a very famous face – the R&B singer Usher!

'[He] was going to the studio the same time as me and I ran up to him as fast as I could,' Justin told the website neonlight.com. Never one to be shy or to miss an opportunity, Justin rushed up to Usher. 'I was like "Usher, Usher! I love your songs! You want me to sing you one?" He gets so many people every day asking him if they can sing for him and give him their demo, so I didn't get to sing for him,' remembered

Justin. Instead, Usher merely held the door open for Justin and said: 'No, little buddy, just come inside, it's cold out.'

Nowadays, Justin loves to tease Usher about how he very nearly let him slip through his fingers. Thankfully, within a week of Usher turning down Justin's offer to sing for him, he saw some of Justin's Internet videos and quickly decided he wanted to sign him. Braun had very helpfully brought along the links to the videos and a sample of the demo Justin had recorded in Atlanta. This time, Usher was impressed. 'Man, I should have let this kid sing,' he said as he finally witnessed Justin's talents. He resolved to do just that and asked Braun to fly Justin – who had since returned to Canada – back to Atlanta.

'I met him again and got to sing for him,' said Justin. Usher was just as impressed by Justin's in-person performance. 'Given my experience, I knew exactly what it would take for him to become an incredible artist,' he said.

No wonder Usher was impressed by Justin's in-person performance that day – Justin sang one of his own songs! Justin chose to sing 'U Got It Bad', which was a Number 1 hit in America for Usher in 2001 and sold well around the world, reaching the Top 5 in the UK and Australia. On the day, Justin was wearing his customary back-to-front baseball cap and a hooded white-and-blue Leafs jumper. As he sang, he casually placed his left hand in his jean pocket and used his right hand to express his feelings.

Halfway through he stopped singing, and cheekily asked Usher: 'You gonna sing it with me, or what?' This was a very confident move for a youngster to try, and Usher was amused and entertained by it. At the end of the song Usher clapped and Pattie made a proud 'Aaahhh' sound, which is clearly heard on the video she filmed of the performance.

Back home in Canada, some of Justin's school friends had not believed him about his fledgling association with the legendary Usher. 'I told everybody, "Yeah, I met Usher," and they were like, "Yeah, right".' It must have been very frustrating for Justin. Knowing the performance was being filmed by Pattie, Usher told Justin: 'Your friends will believe you now.'

Pattie added the video to the YouTube channel, and it has now been watched over 6 million times. It is a little slice of music history because it captures the moment that Usher decided he had to sign Justin to his record label.

So what was Usher's more considered verdict to the performance Justin had given him that day? 'When I met him, his personality just won me over,' he recalled later. 'And then when he sang, I realized we were dealing with the real thing. His voice just spoke to the type of music I would want to be associated with … His voice was magical and his personality was so keen,' said the singer.

He was keen, but Justin was actually quite relaxed about the whole affair. He had arrived with no record deal and the very worst outcome would be that he left in exactly the same position – with no record deal. 'I had nothing, like, to lose,' he explained to an ABC News documentary. 'Like, if I did bad, I wouldn't have gotten a record deal. I was there just having fun. Like, from the start, that was my whole point, you know. If you're not having fun, then why do it?'

It was the same principle he had applied when he entered the Stratford Star competition – and when he busked outside the theatre: most of all he was just aiming to have a fun time. Both of those experiences had, in their different ways, led him to greater success, so the lesson he had learned was that if you keep aiming to enjoy what you're doing, great things can happen. He enjoyed himself when he was singing for Usher and that sense of fun came across. No wonder Usher was so taken by the youngster.

'When I met him, I immediately knew that this kid was poised to be a star,' remembered Usher in the Canadian newspaper *London Free Press*. Usher was also clear that he was the right man to help guide the kid to stardom. 'I knew that I had a lot to offer to him, based off where I'd been. I just wanted to help him tell his story. When I saw him, I just felt like: "You know, this is the one". He's gonna be huge. He's gonna be massive. That's all I can say.'

Usher had no doubt that Justin was a star in the making, nor that he was the man to make that happen for him. The only problem was that he was going to face stiff competition for Justin's signature. With such a hot young prospect on his hands, Braun was no more inclined to offer him to just one label than Pattie had been inclined to take the first managerial offer that had come her way.

By the time Usher had finalized the offer he would put to Justin, Braun had spoken with someone else about the possibility of signing Justin up. That 'someone else' was no ordinary person either: he was the pop sensation Justin Timberlake!

Usher remembered the moment he realized he had a rival for the boy wonder's signature. 'Scooter said, "Justin is interested in this kid",' he recalled. 'I said, "Justin? You mean Justin Timberlake?"' Braun confirmed that this was exactly the case, and that he was going to fly Justin Bieber to California so he could perform for Timberlake.

In truth, all Usher could really do was to sit and hope that his rival did not impress Justin, Pattie and Braun enough to distract them from his own charms. Braun, who was not playing games by bringing a rival into the bidding, explained his reasoning in approaching Timberlake. 'I wanted to bring in another artist to put his stamp on Justin, and Timberlake just signed Esmée Denters to Tennman [Records, Timberlake's label], so I thought he might understand the space. I went to him, and he was 100 per cent in.'

To have Timberlake '100 per cent in' was in itself a huge boost to Justin Bieber's confidence, because if anyone understands what it takes to build and sustain a successful pop career, Justin Timberlake does.

Born on 31 January 1981 in Memphis, Justin Timberlake began his journey to fame early in life. As a child he was known as a 'weenie'. All the same, he enjoyed sport and was a 'point guard' in the school basketball team. So far, so normal – but his life soon became a whole lot more interesting.

He was taking singing lessons when he was just eight years of age and he went on to compete in the American TV talent contest *Star Search*. In 1993 he joined the cast of *The Mickey Mouse Club*, an American television variety show. The show's cast included others who would become massively famous in the future: among his co-stars were Britney Spears and Christina Aguilera.

When *The Mickey Mouse Club* came to an end, Timberlake was in no mood to sit still. Together with some friends he joined a new boy band called 'N Sync. Backed by a great management team, the band quickly won a record deal. They were launched in Germany and became a big hit in Europe before flying up the US charts and becoming a worldwide sensation. Together for seven years, 'N Sync toured the world and had hits across the globe. Although Timberlake loved the fame and fun that came through his place in the band, it was when he launched his solo career in 2002 that he went from becoming a famous pop star to a high-profile celebrity. His first solo album, *Justified*, was released on 5 November 2002. It was a hit, but his second solo effort *FutureSex/LoveSounds* was the real success, and went multi-platinum.

He has won Grammy Awards for his solo material and also became a heart-throb to girls across the globe, topping numerous 'sexiest men' polls. He had a high-profile relationship with Britney Spears and at the 2003 BRIT Awards ceremony he memorably touched the famous behind of pop legend Kylie Minogue during a duet they performed. It was moments like these that made him one of the globe's best-known and most fancied males, an honour now enjoyed by Justin Bieber.

How close Timberlake came to guiding Justin to fame is interesting. One of Timberlake's best-known solo songs is 'Cry Me a River', as covered by Justin Bieber. So when the two Justins met they already had that in common. By this stage Timberlake had set up his own record label, and he quickly became very keen to sign Justin Bieber to it. Before the two Justins met, Braun had told Timberlake all about Justin's talents, and shown him videos and played him demos, 'We had already had it scheduled a week later [following the Usher summit] to go to meet Justin Timberlake, because Justin Timberlake also wanted to sign him, so it almost became like a bidding war between them,' Pattie told a television show. 'Two of the biggest pop stars, you know, wanting be to be involved with, with my little Justin.'

How far 'her little Justin' had come since that fateful day when his YouTube account was opened and the first video uploaded to it! He now had two pop legends keen to sign him to their associated record labels! 'They both kind of wanted me,' as Justin put it. He was excited about this, naturally, and also under no illusions as to what was at stake. 'Justin and Usher are definitely rivals in the industry,' he said. He was amused and surprised to be in the middle of this rivalry, but remained self-assured throughout because he felt it constituted a no-lose situation for him.

'It was just crazy to have two of the biggest pop stars fighting over me,' Justin told *Billboard*. 'Justin was a great guy . . . they're both great. But . . . I mean, you really couldn't have gone wrong either way.'

He enjoyed meeting Timberlake, and also his girlfriend. 'I was really more excited to meet Jessica Biel,' he said of Timberlake's actress girlfriend of the time. 'They invited me to their home, and we watched March Madness [a basketball match].' Fun times, but in the end Justin knew he had a decision to make. He, Pattie and Braun discussed the rival offers. For Pattie this was an important decision to get right for her 'little Justin' who, along with Braun, was just as determined to pick the right deal. They went with Usher.

'It turned out Usher's deal was way better,' said Justin. 'He had L.A. Reid backing him up and Scooter had a lot of really good connections in Atlanta.' It was not the case that he had been unimpressed by Timberlake, he was keen to add. 'I think he's a great guy and I hope to collaborate with him in the future,' said Justin.

Braun was delighted with their choice, because he felt that Justin's signing with a black artist would help get across to the public that though Justin is white, the music he excels at performing is mostly soul music. 'Here's this little white kid singing soul music, from Canada,' said Braun, explaining how easily Justin's style could be misunderstood. 'He needed someone to make people understand that's who he really was.' That someone would be Usher.

Once Usher had been chosen as Justin's mentor, the next step was for Usher to get Justin officially signed to a record label so he could get to work on actual material. This was, perhaps surprisingly, not an entirely easy process, because Justin had met with a degree of scepticism from some industry figures. 'Everyone said "no",' Braun said. 'They said, "He's an incredible singer and an amazing talent, but he's too young and he doesn't have Nickelodeon or Disney behind him."'

Given that many young artists are broken to the American market via either of these two kids' television routes, or if they are a little older they might try the reality television route by auditioning on *American Idol*, Justin did stand out as an exception against these well-established marketing techniques.

Still, though, Braun believed in him. 'I wanted him to be the next Michael Jackson,' he said. 'And literally everyone said no. But his talent was undeniable, and his success is a testament to his true ability.'

However, for some in the industry this was an advantage rather than a disadvantage. Among those was music producer Antonio Reid who, like everyone else at this stage, was instantly impressed when he encountered Justin. 'I thought he was an amazing kid, charming with loads of personality,' recalled Reid, who added that the lack of a TV platform never discouraged him from doing a deal. 'I've never had the benefit of an *American Idol* or Disney type of platform. Maybe it's dated, but we launch artists in the traditional sense. Oftentimes, while these kids may be very talented, we think of them as TV stars first, and the music is secondary. Justin is music first.'

A producer with some very influential music industry connections, Reid was just the sort of person whose approval Justin wanted and needed. Co-founder of a record label called LaFace Records, Ried is also the chairman of the Island Def Jam Music Group. He has been involved in the launch of many well-known pop acts, including Pink, Avril Lavigne and Usher himself, who he signed when he was just fourteen years old. As for Justin, he signed with the label in October 2008.

He had a record deal and was on his way. As Braun vowed, Justin was going to have his career launched a different way. 'Justin's going to be the first artist to become a huge mainstream superstar based on the Internet and not based on anything else,' he said.

How did Justin feel as he stood on the threshold of a new exciting challenge – and how had he arrived where he was? 'I didn't really have plans to get a record deal or anything,' he explained during an interview with *MTV News*. 'I was just – it's kind of like luck, but when it happened I immediately knew that this was what I was born to do.'

Having already been guided brilliantly by his mother and Scooter Braun, Justin knew that having Antonio Reid in his corner was another great advantage. And with Usher as his new mentor, Justin had another great person on his side.

Usher's first piece of advice for Justin was: 'Stay humble and stay on the right path, then anything's possible.' Justin would do his best to stay true to Usher's advice and has proved that the most amazing things *are* possible. As for Usher himself, he was delighted to be working with Justin. He had faced strong competition from Timberlake but had won the day. He said he was in it for the long haul with Justin, who he sees being an artist for a very long time to come. 'Great artists mature with time. To see him now at this age, and think about where he's going to be when he begins to bring real music full circle, when he begins to dictate the sound of the future – I'm looking forward to those days. When I first saw him, I thought about that – I didn't think about how cute he was, or how personable he was, and how much swag he had.'

As he stood on the brink of fame, Justin made his first-ever television appearance. It came on a religious television channel show called *100 Huntley Street*. He was included in a segment of the show called 'Full Circle', in which the guests sit on the sofa and chat. Pattie was alongside him: 'Yeah, actually, Justin is not just healthy like I pray but like I say he's really talented,' she said. 'He's been putting up videos on YouTube and he is now the number one most subscribed-to musician in Canada on YouTube and number twentieth in the world.'

The rest of the female guests then clucked over Justin's singing voice, which they had heard first-hand when he had given them a behind-the-scenes performance before the show. 'He is being courted by the different music labels,' explained Pattie. 'Justin Timberlake and Usher were actually fighting over who could sign him. We've just signed to the music label and we're moving, in about a week, to the US, so it's a big step. He's got a long journey and great plans.'

As the panel moved on to the next item, one of them said Justin's life was a 'Cinderella story'. It certainly does have something of that fairy tale about it – and there were so many people performing the role of the 'fairy godmother' that Justin's experience was about to get even more wondrous. He would not be just *going* to the ball – pretty soon Justin would be the *star* of it.

There was a lot of excitement on the horizon for Justin. It is possibly just as well that he never dreamed of a pop career because not even the most imaginative dreamer could have conjured up what would happen next . . .

5

One Time

As he set off on his journey to fame, Justin was excited, but he also had some doubts about where he was headed. Everything was happening very quickly, so it is perfectly understandable that he was anxious about what lay ahead for him. In fact, in one so young, it would be strange if he did not have mixed feelings at this stage. 'At first, I didn't know if this is what I wanted,' he confided.

However, given the extrovert personality he had shown all his life and the extraordinary confidence he exuded when performing, it was not long before he realized that it was, indeed, what he wanted. 'I really love to be in the spotlight,' he concluded, 'and just be the centre of the attention.' Well, once he released his first single he would be the centre of the whole world's attention. However, first he had to record it.

Although he had recorded a demo during his initial meet-ups with Scooter Braun, this was to be the first time for Justin working in a 'proper' recording studio. Imagine what an exciting day it must have been for him when he first walked into a big studio, full of instruments, gadgets and other interesting musical items: he was finally arriving where he knew he belonged. He was determined to work hard and prove himself!

Justin was in good hands. He worked with leading music producers and songwriters like Terius 'The-Dream' Nash, Tricky Stewart, Bryan-Michael Cox, Johnta Austin and Kuk Harrell. They taught him a lot – and taught him fast. 'It was my first time ever being in the studio,' Justin remembered with happiness. 'I think my emotion has always been there, but I know what to do better now, and my voice has developed.' Justin played around at times, but he was keen to learn and knew when the time to play was over and the time for work began.

Helping him along in the studio at times was the experienced figure of Usher. However, Usher's guidance went far beyond just matters of music. He was in all senses an example to Justin, for whom he felt very responsible. 'He's very protective of Justin,' explained Braun. 'He sees himself at that age, and he doesn't want Justin making any of the mistakes he made. He wants Justin to win. And one of the best things about having Usher as part of the team, is that he will understand what Justin is going through. To have that outlet for Justin is invaluable and really a blessing.'

When asked how his relationship with his musical mentor was progressing, Justin was just as upbeat. 'He's like a big brother to me,' Justin said of Usher. 'We just hang out and don't really talk about music a lot. We go go-karting and to arcades and movies.' It was as if Usher was taking on the mantle that had previously been held by Chad Ritter, who had driven to Stratford to entertain Justin when he was much younger. Usher also gave Justin important advice as his career developed and his fame soared. Without the attention and help of someone who had himself experienced what it was like to become suddenly famous at a very young age, the process would have been much harder for Justin to face.

One of the big changes that Justin had to make was where he lived. It quickly became clear that he would need to live in America, as that was where he was doing most of his work. So he and Pattie packed their things and took them to Atlanta. He found it fairly easy to settle in, but he did notice differences between his new home and the town he had left behind in Canada. 'In my town, there were only 30,000 people, but in Atlanta there are millions,' he told *MTV News*. 'And I don't know anybody [in Atlanta], but everybody knows everybody in my town in Canada.'

In these new surroundings he learned quickly and grew as a singer while also – literally – growing as a human being. He was going through the usual changes that boys in their teenage years face, while also having to get his head around the fact that the public were becoming increasingly aware of him. True, the fame he had at this stage was relatively minor compared to the superstardom he enjoys now. But back then it was huge and real enough to test him.

Having worked on a lot of material in the studio, the song chosen as his first single, the release that would 'officially' launch his career, was written by the experienced songwriting partnership of Tricky Stewart and Terius 'The-Dream' Nash. They had been writing together for years, particularly producing songs in the hip-hop and R&B genres. They were involved in the writing of the song 'Umbrella', which was such a hit for the soul singer Rihanna. The song has won a Grammy Award and went to Number 1 in many countries including the UK, USA and France. They also wrote Beyoncé's 'Single Ladies (Put a Ring on It)', which was another hit around the world and chosen by *Rolling Stone* magazine as one of its favourite singles of 2008. Stewart had also helped write hits for Britney Spears, Mariah Carey and Jesse McCartney. So the writing of Justin's first single was in very good hands.

The song they wrote and chose for him was called 'One Time', and the whole team agreed that this was the best song to choose as Justin's first release. It begins with a beat and chant that is similar to the one used for Rihanna for 'Umbrella' and that has been used for hip-hop songs too. However, rather than a gravelly rapper's voice coming in, instead listeners were treated to the sweet, high voice of Justin singing 'Me, plus you' three times in a strict chant. He then continues to sing the lyrics that declare his love for the girl at the centre of the song. The song is about the importance of the girl to his life. She is his one and only love for the rest of his life. Of course, this struck a chord with his fans, many of whom dream of being such a girl! The intense lyrics go on to paint him and the girl as an unbreakable partnership, their world, their fight, their breath are all shared.

These sorts of feelings were ones that Justin enjoyed bringing into song. 'I love singing about love,' he explained to *Twist* magazine. 'That's what a lot of girls like listening to, and that's what I like to write.' From singer to fan – it was the start of a great relationship.

All the same, his concentration on this theme posed questions in the minds of some observers. From the start of his career, Justin has sometimes been asked just how much a boy of his age really understands about love. To be fair, the people who ask him about this probably knew more about love when they were Justin's age than they remember now. In any case, Justin is clear that sometimes when younger people think they are in 'real' love, it is a different kind of love they are experiencing. '"One Time" is basically about being in a typical teen relationship, so it's a song everyone can relate to,' he told the Digital Spy website. 'You know when you're younger and you thought it was love, but then later on you realize it was just puppy love? That's what the song's about.' This showed great maturity and awareness on Justin's part – and suggested that he was more than ready to sing about these themes.

When Justin was recording the song, Usher made a short video that was added to Justin's ongoing YouTube channel. The video begins with Justin in the recording booth, singing the chorus of the song into the microphone. Usher stops the backing track that Justin is singing to and pops into the booth. He says to the camera: 'I'm going to stop you like that because this is just a tease. Ladies and gentlemen, introducing to you Island Def Jam's recording artist Justin Bieber, he's getting ready to go down. Just so you know we in the studio right now working on it. Get ready, cos it going to be big. Ain't that right, Justin?' 'That's right,' says Justin in a slightly croaky voice. Then Usher concludes the short video saying: 'So look out – we coming!'

The single was indeed coming – and everyone in Justin's team was superconfident that they had done a great job with it!

The choice of the song was paramount. The first single to be released from any forthcoming album is important because it is the best way of developing interest in the album. When you add in the fact that this was Justin's first ever CD release, it was vitally important that everything was perfect. The production team did a great job on the mixing of the song. Everyone they had tested it on was impressed, as Justin's manager explained. 'People don't hear it and think, "Oh, it's a little kid's record",' said Braun. 'He's a young kid who sings with a lot more soul than he should.'

As for Justin, his ultimate words on the single were: 'It's just a fun pop record, and it's a song that the girls definitely like.'

The song was handed to American radio stations in May 2009, ready for official release to the public in July. All Justin and his team could do was sit with their fingers – and possibly toes! – crossed, hoping it would be a success. They could hardly wait to learn what the critics would think of the song and – even more importantly – how well it would sell.

While they waited for its release, Justin and his team added another video to his YouTube channel. This one featured Justin sitting in a car with actor, comedian and rapper Nick Cannon. 'What's the deal, y'all?' said Cannon at the start of the recording. 'I'm here with the future right now,' he added, referring to Justin. 'The future of everything, the future of entertainment – JB aka Justin Bieber!' He then explains that they are driving in Hollywood and that earlier they had faced some *paparazzi* photographers. The video then shows Cannon introducing Justin to a gang of photographers, whose cameras are soon flashing wildly at Justin – for whom this onslaught was a whole new experience. He would soon get more used to them.

'It ain't even about me,' Cannon tells the press pack. 'It's about him – ask Usher!'

The video then returns to the calm of the car where Cannon explains to the camera that he and Justin have just been eating a sushi meal. 'But [Justin] didn't go too hard, he's like me – we didn't go too hard on the sushi. We tried California Rolls.' Justin then explains to the camera that he is in Los Angeles to shoot the video for his first single. Referring to the single, Cannon says: 'Which is on fire! That joint is crazy! I'm banging it in the club already.'

Soon after this one, Justin added another video to his YouTube channel so he could send a further message to his fans as the countdown to the release of his first single continued. 'Wassup, guys, this is Justin Bieber,' he said. 'I just wanted to thank you guys for all your support you've been truly amazing. I wouldn't be in this position without you.'

He explained he had been driving around doing 'promo' for his single, and that he had opened an account on the social networking website Facebook, in addition to his accounts on Twitter and MySpace, and, of course, his YouTube channel. 'So just check it out and thanks a lot for your support,' he said, bringing the video to an end.

The single release was just around the corner. As he counted the days to that release, Justin dreamt of what reaction it might receive . . .

On release, the media was very positive in its verdict. It was, after all, a truly brilliant song – and who could fail to be charmed by the story of the kid from Canada who was discovered through YouTube? In *Billboard*, Michael Menachem wrote that 'One Time' 'gives Bieber's vocals plenty of room to shine, especially when the young singer confidently breaks into the chorus, connecting overtly with his fans'.

The VNU Entertainment News Wire said the single was 'a hallmark pop song that also taps into a prevalent teen hip-hop aesthetic'. It predicted that Justin, 'already an online sensation, will most certainly only grow from here, as first-time listeners rush to discover the boy behind the voice'. That review, and the one published in the *Toronto Star*, compared Justin with the singer Chris Brown at the same age.

The Canadian press described 'One Time' as a 'hip-hop-inflected pop single'. Bill Lamb, writing on the website About.com, called it a 'perfect kick-off to the career of Justin Bieber', while in *Entertainment Weekly* Leah Greenblatt concluded that in the song Justin 'earns his pop-soul bona fides with this refreshingly age-appropriate chronicle of young love'. As for the BBC website, it too was impressed: 'Its thudding beat and syrupy message . . . are perfect ingredients for mainstream appeal'.

The single was a hit in the charts but Justin had to wait a little while before he could celebrate as it was not an instant hit. It began at Number 95 in America's all-important *Billboard* Top 100 and reached the Top 25 of that chart. In Justin's homeland of Canada it performed even better in the charts, reaching Number 12. It also sold well in Europe, including in the UK, France, Austria and Germany. In New Zealand, meanwhile, 'One Time' reached Number 6. It finished at number 89 on the 2009 *Billboard* end-of-year Top 100, and 81 in the equivalent chart in Canada.

Justin was excited by his early success and never more so than when he learned that 'One Time' had gone platinum in Canada – meaning it had sold at least 10,000 copies in that country alone. He will always remember the day when he received news of this exciting honour. Justin was on a fun day out at Canada's Wonderland, a popular amusement park in Toronto. Early in the evening on Sunday 27 September 2009 he took a phone call and was told of the platinum status of his debut single. He couldn't wait to share the news with his growing following on the Twitter website. '2nite was incredible,' he wrote. 'I got surprised with my first Canadian Platinum plaque for "One Time"! I will never forget 2nite.'

Part of what had helped the song become successful was the brilliant promotional video that accompanied its release. Again, this was a hugely important thing to get right because, as the video that launched Justin to the world, it was the first real chance to show the world what sort of singer and person Justin was. This was the video that would shape his image, which is all-important in the entertainment world of the twenty-first century. Justin's raw, home-made YouTube videos had worked very well for him, but now was the time to introduce him to a wider audience with a more professional package. We all know first impressions count, so they *had* to get it right.

Luckily, Justin is not the sort of person who feels pressure when he's working on things like this: he was, as ever, too busy enjoying himself! 'It was really cool going from my webcam to professional videos,' he said. As we have seen, while he was filming the video he had fun meeting up with Nick Cannon and trying some sushi. But as well as the fun there was lots of work to be done too.

Vashtie Kola was hired to be director of the video. She had begun her career as a video director before L.A. Reid hired her to become director of Creative Services at Island Def Jam. Kola's role at the record company was a wide-ranging one, and included being 'the one to keep the building cool, someone in tune with downtown cool and pop mainstream'. She is indeed a cool and stylish person, so much so that *Vibe* magazine once named her as one of its '31 Most Stylish People Under 31', which featured some very highly esteemed names to be alongside – including Kanye West and Justin Timberlake! She was excited to land the job of directing the video for Justin's debut single. 'He's super-talented and more street than any of these child stars,' she said as she flew to Los Angeles for the shoot.

Justin adored her, and the feeling was mutual. They chatted about skateboarding and Justin mentioned what a huge fan he is of Terry Kennedy. Sometimes known as Compton Ass Terry or TK, Kennedy is a popular professional skateboarder. When Kola realized that Justin was a fan, she said she: 'Called up the homie and asked him for a solid,' meaning she invited him to visit Justin. 'He was more than happy to come through, Terry is the sweetest dude – seriously,' she recalled. He did indeed 'come through', wearing a huge chain around his neck with TK attached to it. He showed the excited Justin some new skateboarding tricks. 'Terry gave him some skating pointers on tricks that Justin was trying to master, and within moments Justin was killing it,' wrote Kola on her website.

The video was shot at Usher's large house. For Justin, this was an immediate opportunity to see the sort of extravagant lifestyle that can follow from pop success. As he looked around Usher's home he was impressed and more than a little excited.

The video begins with Justin and his friend Ryan sitting on Usher's sofa playing a computer game. Justin has just got one over his friend and smiles as he says: 'That was not luck, that was skill!' As they continue playing Justin's phone rings and we see from the phone's flashing screen that it is Usher on the line! Then we see Usher sitting in a different location. 'JB – what's up, man?' he asks. 'I'm just playing video games with Ryan,' explains Justin. Usher then asks if Justin can look after the house until he gets home. 'Yeah, I can do that,' replies Justin. 'All right, my man,' says Usher.

At the end of the phone call, Justin turns to Ryan with a mischievous grin. Nobody does cheeky as well as Justin! Soon the duo are texting their friends, inviting them to a party at Usher's house. Naturally, there are plenty of takers and before long the house and the garden are full of kids happily dancing and partying. For Justin, however, there is only one girl that interests him at the party, in keeping with the lyrics that sing about the 'one girl' in his imagination. He spends the party with her; they chat and hug in the kitchen and are also seen later sitting on a bench by the pool. He is paying all his attention to her and making her feel special. They may have been acting, but the actress in that video would soon be the envy of girls across the planet. Particularly for the scene when Justin gives her a kiss on the cheek.

The video ends with a moment of cheeky comedy. As Justin walks towards the house from the garden he walks straight into Usher, who has arrived back at the home he asked Justin to guard. Usher looks around at the busy party scene and Justin turns to the camera with a cheeky smile before running off.

Throughout the party scenes in the video, shots of Justin singing alone into the camera are cut in regularly. These are professionally shot scenes but for those fans who had followed Justin since before he was officially famous, they are familiar. As he sings to the camera he makes great use of his hands to express his emotions and points, just as he did on many of his home-made YouTube videos. All in all, the video for 'One Time' is very entertaining and it was perfect to launch Justin as a great singer, as well as a cute and cheeky character.

Ever the fun-lover and performer, Justin enjoyed working on his first promotional video enormously. 'It was really crazy, but it was an amazing experience!' he told neonlimelight.com. Asked how he felt having Usher on the set with him, he replied: 'Well, I mean, to be honest, a lot of people have been asking like, "It must be amazing to hang out with Usher," but he's just a regular cat like you and me, so it's just like hanging out with anybody else. But it's cool. It's cool to have one of my inspirations on set.'

He was also delighted that he was able to include his best friend to play a part in the video. 'Yes, that's my best friend, Ryan," he told *Tiger Beat*. 'We've been friends since we were little. We played hockey together and went to school together.' Another of the joys of the video for Justin was that he was allowed to take part in the casting of some of the female parts – including the girl who took the lead part alongside him in the later stages of the video! 'Yes, they let me pick,' he confirmed happily. 'I like a girl with a nice smile and eyes.'

When the video first hit the airwaves on 12 June 2009, plenty of girls liked what they saw. They were even more excited the following month when Justin launched a related competition via his YouTube channel. No wonder they were excited – the winner of the competition got to meet Justin! In the video that announced the competition, Justin was sitting in the back of a car. He was, he explained, 'Chilling out, kinda driving down the freeway'. He then explained how the competition would work. 'This right here is the official contest video,' he said. 'I'm having a contest to see who can make the most creative video promoting my single "One Time". The winner will be able to fly out to meet me, with a friend. We'll just hang out and have a good time. You have all of July to do it, so either go big or go home. Justin Bieber signing off.'

It was a happy day for the winner of the competition when they found out they had got lucky. The winners were two fans called Lyndsay and Ali.

Justin's YouTube channel was proving to be a very useful tool in promoting his career. When his video was first placed on the iTunes store he announced this via his channel. On 23 June he uploaded a video in which he said: 'Wassup guys, this is Justin Bieber. My music video is officially on iTunes so make sure you guys go and buy it.' As Braun explained, he was encouraging Justin to use YouTube more so he could show his fans that they had a special connection with him. 'I wanted to build him up more on YouTube first. We supplied more content. I said: "Justin, sing like there's no one in the room. But let's not use expensive cameras." We'll give it to kids, let them do the work, so that they feel like it's theirs.'

This connection between Justin and his fans was seen again in another online contest arranged in September 2009. Justin announced the contest via his MySpace blog. 'What do you have to do? It's simple – Upload a video of yourself explaining or showing why you are [my] BIGGEST fan to Your.Mtv.Com.' The prize was that the winner would receive a mention from Justin when he was at the MTV Music Awards.

'Being able to have them all participate just makes me feel good,' said Justin of bringing his fans closer to him again in a chat with *MTV News*. 'Having them make videos for me is awesome. I mean, without my fans, I wouldn't be here, so I definitely am thankful for my fans. You guys keep coming up with the videos. They're awesome, so just keep them coming.'

This time the winner was a fan called Tricia Matibag from Ottawa. 'I was so happy,' she told *MTV News*. 'I called my best friend because she is, like, a fan. She was just at my house and I was screaming really loud! I love [Justin] and it made my whole entire year!' Asked why she loved Justin so much Tricia said: 'I love that he's just a normal guy that came from Canada like me and his dream came true. Also he's really cute and an amazing singer.' No wonder she was so excited to win!

Soon after the release of 'One Time', Justin had the sort of milestone that only a pop star like Justin can expect to have in life – the first time he heard his music on the radio! 'I was in the car,' he told Disney *Total Access*. 'I was changing the channel and I was like, "What?" and I turned back. I was with my mom and we were, like, jamming out. I thought, "This is, this is pretty weird!" We listened to it for a couple of seconds and then I changed it!' It was an exciting moment for Justin but perhaps even then he realized that this was something he would soon get used to.

In the meantime, on the horizon he had an album to release, but before it even came out Justin was already amazing the music industry and setting a new record when he became the first solo artist to have four songs from a debut album appear in the *Billboard*'s Hot 100 *prior* to the album even

Justin's a hit all over the world, including: Paris (left), Sydney (bottom) and New York (below).

Hard at work: Justin in London (facing page, above); at the *Late Show with David Letterman* (facing page, below); in his native Canada at the Juno Awards (above); and walking the red carpet at the White House Correspondents' Association Dinner in Washington (left).

Yet it's not all work and no play. Justin kicks back at the Six Flags Magic Mountain in California (top); during a bowling game in New York (above); on the beach in Sydney (facing page: above, and below left); and on a bungee jump in New Zealand (facing page, below right).

Raw talent: Justin wows the crowd at the Wango Tango Concert in LA.

Beat it: performing on Miami Beach.

Superstar: singing at the BBC Radio 1 Big Weekend in Bangor, Wales.

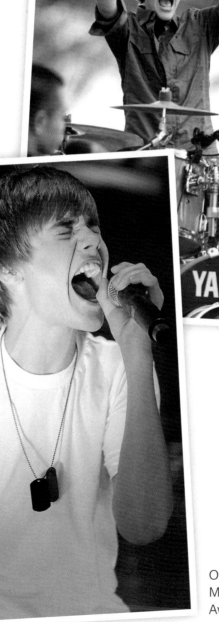

Overleaf: At the MuchMusic Video Awards in Toronto.

being released.

To have set a new music industry record at such a tender age and so early in his career showed again what a bright future Justin has ahead of him. Many pop singers have careers that run for years – even decades – without breaking such a significant record. Here was Justin doing it while still a teenage boy.

The first of these four fateful songs was, of course, 'One Time'. It was followed on 6 October by 'One Less Lonely Girl', a sweet and mid-tempo song that kicks off with Justin saying: 'Okay, let's go.' He then sings about the heartaches, loneliness and disappointments that the female subject of the song has experienced, and promises that he will bring them all to an end. He promises that he will put her first and show her what her worth is. If only, he sings, she lets him into her world, then he will make sure she is never lonely again. The final flourish of the song comes at the end when Justin says: 'Only you shawty' and giggles.

It is a great song, which many fans still consider is Justin's best song to date. It was co-written by Justin's mentor and friend Usher, alongside other songwriters including Ezekiel Lewis. A heartfelt and catchy pop classic, it was loved by fans and critics alike. Crystal Bell of *Billboard* was very impressed. 'Much as he did on his debut single, "One Time", Bieber makes a strong case for why he's the next pop/R&B heart-throb,' she wrote. '"I'm gonna put you first, I'll show you what you're worth/If you let me inside your world," he sings. The stump speech is hard to resist, especially when set to an arrangement that follows the lineage of hit mid-tempo ballads "With You", and "Irreplaceable". Although the lyrics are generic, Bieber's smooth delivery is right on point, and his tender vocals blend well with the song's easy-flowing beat.' They do indeed!

Justin also loves the song and the message it gives to his female fans. 'I think it's really important these girls have something so they can be one less lonely girl,' he told *MTV News*.

The promotional video is very entertaining. It features Justin becoming besotted by a girl he sees at a launderette. As he sits there with his acoustic guitar, he notices a girl doing her washing – and likes what he sees! He and the girl share some shy and cheeky smiles and then she leaves. But as she does so she accidentally leaves her red scarf behind. Justin picks up the scarf, has a quick think, and breaks into a huge smile. No wonder he is happy – he has found a way to get close to the girl of his dreams!

The rest of the video features his quest to win her affections. He leaves arrows on the street, pointing her to him and also leaves photographs of himself so she can see it was he who left the arrows. When she next arrives at the laundry she looks around for him but he's not there. She is disappointed at first but then finds the first note left by Justin. 'I have your scarf', the note tells her. 'If you want it back, find me!' As she follows Justin's trail of notes she finds they include romantic promises. Now she is even more interested and continues to follow the trail.

As the video continues, her next stop is outside a pet shop. There, Justin had earlier been photographed surrounded by

cute puppies. He sure knows how to win a girl's heart! The
note he has left here includes the photographs and alongside
them a written promise to shower her with kisses. No
wonder she keeps following the arrows. They then lead her
to a flower stall where his next note promises he will give
her flowers and another saying he will 'make every moment
magical'! Finally, she finds Justin back at the laundry. He is
wearing a short-sleeved white shirt and a blue T-shirt and
he hands her back her red scarf. Of course, this is not the
end of the story and the two soon cuddle and dance as the
video comes to an end. Sweet, entertaining and romantic,
the video was perfect and did justice to the themes of
the song.

As Justin revealed on *MTV News*, he had worked with an
experienced man in the making of the video. 'I actually shot
[the video] with Roman White, who directed "You Belong
With Me" by Taylor Swift,' he said. 'So it's going to be a lot
of fun.' Taylor Swift is an American singer who performs
country and pop style songs. Her career would coincide with
Justin's again in the future.

As for White, he has a great pedigree in video making,
having produced many for *American Idol* winner Carrie
Underwood. He was determined to make the whole
experience fun for Justin. Although pop videos are only

around four minutes long, they can take many days or even weeks to make. While Justin is delighted to have a pop career and is more than willing to work hard, everyone on his team was aware that he was a young boy and would need to be entertained throughout the process.

They need not have worried. As he worked on the video Justin's sense of fun was again bubbling to the surface. Wearing a green hooded jumper and a pink T-shirt, he looked fantastic as he shot the outdoor scenes. Some of the walls had been painted the same shade of pink as his T-shirt, which gave the filming a great colour quality. As he sang the 'one' in the chorus, he performed his trademark holding up of one finger.

The video was filmed in Watertown, Tennessee, a small, friendly town and as a location it gave the video a nice colourful and innocent feel. A small-town boy himself, Justin was delighted when he arrived in the town. Looking at his surroundings he joked, 'This like the biggest town I've ever been in, seriously!' On a more serious note he added: 'No, it's really small and quaint and cute and cool. Everyone probably knows everybody I guess.' He was enjoying the experience, and told the crew who were recording a 'behind-the-scenes' video: 'I'm really excited.'

When they shot the scene at the pet shop, Justin loved cuddling up with the cute puppies. The puppies got rather excited too – a little too much in one case. One of the cute puppies relieved itself over Justin. 'There was a pee issue at one point,' confirmed Roman White with a grin. It was only a minor leak and the problem was soon cleaned up so filming could continue. Justin still adored the puppies – he's a forgiving boy!

In another behind-the-scenes chat, Justin explained what the 'dog tag' necklace he was wearing meant to him. This necklace has since become almost as much of a trademark to Justin's image as has his famous hairstyle. 'Actually, a fan gave it to me,' he said. 'And they said it was a very close friend of theirs that was in the war and it was actually his and he passed away. So I wear it because it's kind of cool and it's a kind of memory.' He has also said that he wears it 'for the fans'.

Back on-set, during some banter between takes, director White teased Justin about the cameo appearance in the video made by his mother Pattie. 'For some reason Justin has to have his mother in every one of his videos,' White said. 'Because he loves his mother and that's cool to love your mother!' Justin agreed with half of what White had said. 'It's cool to love your mother,' he confirmed, 'but I don't have to have her in every one of my videos.' After many hours of work, the filming of the video finally came to an end. As filming finished, Justin felt very happy. He lifted his guitar into the air and shouted: 'Done!'

The video went down a treat with Justin's fans. So many of them had dreamed of being romanced by their hero that it was fun for them to watch it being played out on screen. They could dream that one day they might be in the shoes of the female actress! The MTV blog 'Buzzworthy' was impressed. Noting the small-town location for the video they thought it was well chosen. 'And why not? Is this kid not the slice of apple pie cooling on the window sill of the American teen dream?' After noting how nicely-kept the laundry is, the blog concluded: 'There's some lost-and-found action with a scarf that eventually leads to some young love. Your heart, it is warmed.'

The AOL website loved it too, and writer Stacey Hinojosa made it clear what she thought the highlight of the video was: 'and then, as if the video couldn't get more cute, they bring out the puppies'.

Justin kept true to his Internet roots when he chose to premiere the video on a celebrity blogger website. 'He's the hottest tween phenomenon on the planet right now,' wrote blogger Perez Hilton as he unveiled the video on his website. It was then released onto iTunes and shown on YouTube, as well as Justin's official website.

The third single to form the quartet of hits that preceded his album release was called "Love Me". This was a digital-only release, only available to buy via download rather than on a physical CD. It is an upbeat track that samples in the chorus another well-known pop tune.

In 1996 a band called The Cardigans released a catchy song called 'Lovefool'. It became a hit record and was used on the soundtrack of a popular film, *Romeo + Juliet*. As Justin's fans listened to "Love Me", some of their older relatives pricked up one ear and wondered whether they had heard the song before!

Entertainment Weekly certainly approved of his sampling of The Cardigans' song, saying with approval how 'he riffs on the Cardigans' "Lovefool" atop a killer electro-glam groove'. MTV described it as 'a widescreen club track that is full of bubbly synths and Bieber's now-signature croon'. The BBC made a similar observation, describing the song as 'an electro-infused reinterpretation of The Cardigans' "Lovefool", where Bieber exhibits the right kind of attitude, playful and endearing'.

The choice of the third single came as a bit of a shock to Justin himself originally. He had thought that the song would be an acoustic version of 'One Time' and announced this on his Twitter feed. However, after the change of plan he announced: 'NEW SONG – NEVER BEFORE HEARD – HITTING ITUNES NEXT TUESDAY – WHAT IS IT CALLED??? "LOVE ME" – u excited???? spread the word'. He was also taken a little unawares by the release date of 26 October, a day earlier than he had expected. 'Its true,' he wrote on Twitter. 'LOVE ME is out a day early on ITUNES. Im surprised 2. Just bought it. Please support. still sick. thanks for all the well wishes.'

Although it was only released for digital download, 'Love Me' sold well. It reached Number 12 in the Canadian charts and number 37 in the American chart, also charting in Britain and Australia as Justin's fame and popularity spread round the globe like wildfire. People everywhere were starting to realize what a great talent – and guy – he is!

The fourth single to be unleashed ahead of his album release was another love song called 'Favorite Girl'. Of all his singles to date, this one was arguably the most uptempo. It brought in R&B flavours and had a notable synthesizer, giving it a more modern feel than some of his other songs. It was written by a team of songwriters including Antea Birchett and Delisha Thomas.

The song first emerged during a memorable YouTube head-to-head between Justin and Taylor Swift. First, Swift posted a tour diary onto the video-sharing website. The diary used Justin's song 'One Time' as its soundtrack. When he was tipped off about it by one of his fans, Justin thought this was amusing and exciting. 'I watched it and it was hilarious,' he said. 'She was mouthing the words!' Justin was keen to make a fast, online response. So, as a 'reaction' video, he posted a recording of him playing 'Favorite Girl' acoustically.

It was a video that was deliberately light-hearted and humorous. 'Justin "Johnny Cash" Bieber presents Favorite Girl,' said the opening text. 'Wassup guys?' says Justin, who is wearing dark glasses and sitting with his guitar alongside another guitarist, at the start of the video. 'Bieber Cash, here,' he adds, then pointing at the camera, 'This song, right here, is dedicated to you – Taylor Swift . . . This is a song I've never played for anybody. Only to you. It's called "Favorite Girl", cos you are my favorite girl. Justin Cash, Bieber Cash. Let's do it.'

He then sings and plays the song, accompanied by his own guitar and that of his older co-guitarist. As the song finishes Justin walks close to the camera and says: 'Bieber

Cash, Cash Money, Taylor Swift – peace'. The sign-off text at the end of the video reassured any fans who had felt a little jealous by his online serenading of Swift. 'Don't worry, ladies you're all my "Favorite Girl" hahaha,' it read.

Smart move, Justin!

He uploaded the video on 20 August 2009. On the accompanying text, he wrote: 'Hey guys it's me, Justin. I saw Taylor Swift used my song in her last video and was singing it with all her friends having fun and being silly, so I decided to have some fun of my own and make this as a response. This is one of my alter egos Bieber Cash . . . haha . . . (johnny cash, get it? No? ok :P) The song is "Favorite Girl" off my upcoming album *My World*. Hope you guys like it. Spread the word. Thanks – Justin.'

That was the story behind the song, but it was not until November that Justin officially released a studio version of it. On that day he marked the release by performing on *The Ellen DeGeneres Show*. This is the top daytime talk show in America, hosted by the comedian who has since also become a judge on the reality television show *American Idol* – and it is a *very* big deal to be invited to appear on the show.

As she introduced her guest, DeGeneres said: 'Our next guest has a mind-boggling 80 million views on YouTube and he's only fifteen years old. Here to make his daytime television debut, please welcome the adorable Justin Bieber.' Wearing a green checked shirt, Justin appeared on the stage and sang a medley of his songs. He began with some unaccompanied lines from 'Favorite Girl' and then moved to 'One Time', complete with backing track and singers. It was an energetic performance and the audience was soon on its feet, dancing along. The hostess, meanwhile, smiled with approval at how Justin was lighting up the atmosphere in the studio. Due to an injury Ellen herself was unable to dance – but it was obvious from her face that she wanted to.

'I just wanna say that I've never felt older in my life,' she said as Justin joined her for an interview. 'Normally I would be all over the place jumping up and down . . . You couldn't be more adorable.' She then referred to the 'overflow' section of the audience, those who turned up to be in the studio but were unable to gain entry. This overflow section was bursting with Justin's excited female fans, and DeGeneres invited two of them in to sit in the front row – just yards from their heart-throb. Lucky girls!

DeGeneres asked Justin how he was discovered and he told her the story of how he started by uploading videos onto YouTube to share with his friends and family. 'I guess it just kind of blew up,' he added. She asked him what advice Usher had given him. 'Definitely just to stay humble,' said Justin. 'That's probably the most important thing. If I just stay humble and stay on the right path – anything's possible.'

'Exactly,' the hostess agreed. 'You have the talent, you have the charisma, you're just as cute as you could be – you couldn't be cuter. I mean you may be peaking right now – be careful. That's how cute you are – I couldn't imagine you getting cuter. But . . . this business is crazy, a rollercoaster, so stay really grounded.'

DeGeneres went on to talk about how many female fans he had and how devoted they were to him. 'And you have confidence, not cockiness, and I like that. Cos cockiness is arrogant and obnoxious, but you're very confident.' She then turned to the recent newspaper rumours that Justin had asked out the pop sensation Rihanna. The rumour, if true, it would certainly be one that proved he was 'very confident' so it was a good time to ask the question!

'Did you ask Rihanna out? Is that true?' she asked him. 'Yes, that did happen. I just went in,' Justin replied with a proud smile. The audience laughed at the thought of a cute fifteen-year-old kid asking out a successful woman in her twenties. 'And what did Rihanna say?' wondered the hostess. 'I'm not dating her,' Justin replied. 'But I will be friendly with her,' he added. 'Maybe in a few years …' DeGeneres agreed, saying, 'Maybe she'll date you later. You never know!' She was clearly charmed by her young guest.

DeGeneres invited Justin to say hello to the two fans – Kirsten and Laura – who had been chosen to join the studio from the overflow. He walked over, much to their excitement, and said, 'How are ya?' He then shook both girls by the hand and agreed to sign their merchandise. When one of the girls nervously dropped her pen, Justin leant down to pick it up for her. What a gentleman!

His first appearance on daytime television had gone

brilliantly and he had won a whole new set of fans among the key audience who watched the show, many of whom are older than his key fan base. Who could fail to have been charmed by him as he chatted with DeGeneres?

The MTV website was quick to express how much their team had enjoyed the interview with the headline, 'Justin Bieber Charms On *Ellen*, Debuts New Single'. The website also loved the new single, calling it, 'a funky, groovy, swaggerific jam'. When he performed the song live it was obvious how popular it was. After that one performance, *The New York Times* described 'Favorite Girl' as, 'his best song of the night'.

Considering that it was a digital-only release, 'Favorite Girl' sold well and hit the Top 30 in America and the Top 20 in Canada. It completed the four singles to chart ahead of the release of the album they were taken from. These were extraordinary times, and Justin could hardly believe what was happening to him. But if he thought that the devotion and excitement he was generating among his fans was already big, he had hardly seen the half of it. Justin Bieber was about to see his fame and popularity rocket as he took his next steps in an amazing career.

The next step would be the release of his first album – and he wasn't even sixteen years old yet . . .

6

His World

t was while preparing for the release of *My World* that Justin began to see what a frenzy of excitement his pop career had provoked among young girls. His management team was keen for him to do plenty of promotional work before the album release, and they did not have to work hard to convince the media to feature Justin.

Indeed, it would have been physically impossible for Justin to fulfil all of the requests that came his way – he was a young guy in hot demand! Those that he did take on were exciting experiences for him. He was still getting used to the everyday business of being a celebrity. As he travelled round several countries to promote *My World* he was given many strong and some unexpected reminders of just how popular he was.

For instance, when he visited the Canadian cable television station Much Music in July a huge crowd of girls queued up to see him. Many had waited over five hours for the chance to get a glimpse of him, and as they waited they sang the lyrics to 'One Time' and chanted for their boy. This was a sign of true devotion! As they sang and chanted they waved banners with messages about Justin. One read, 'I love Justin', another said, 'You give me the Bieber fever'. Another was held by a girl who had written, 'I go for younger guys!' Well, that was honest and to the point!

When the 'younger guy' of the hour appeared in the studio he was wearing a light blue hooded top and dark blue jeans. As he appeared he naturally prompted a huge scream from the fans. The screams went on after he had been interviewed. Justin was keen to see as many of his fans as possible and stepped outside the studio to meet and greet those who were lined up outside. He could hardly believe so many people had turned up just to see him – what a crowd!

He signed as many autographs as he could and posed for photographs with fans whenever possible. Meanwhile they chanted, screamed and pushed harder to try and get his attention. He sang along with them too. It was obvious from this early stage that Justin truly knew how to 'work a crowd'. This is a great natural skill for any star to have – many are too awkward to pull it off.

Even when he was finished for the day the fans still lined the streets around the studio, screaming with excitement at the knowledge that their idol was in their midst. As he left for the day he ran across to give them one final wave, then popped his hood over his head and jumped into the van that whisked him away.

A highlights video of the day was shot by his team and added to his YouTube channel. He left a special message on his YouTube channel to thank his fans. 'Hey guys it's Justin . . . I just wanted to add a note thanking you personally for all the support,' it read. 'You are helping a kid from a small town chase a dream and I am forever grateful. Thanks to you my family is having a chance at a better life and I am getting to go and see places I could have never dreamed of. This is just the beginning but I wanted to let you know how thankful I am because without you this would never have happened.'

He might have become part of the 'mainstream' pop industry, but, just as Usher had advised him, Justin was 'keeping it real' when it came to remembering his roots. He had been discovered via YouTube and had an army of fans there before he even got a record deal, so he was determined to retain his Internet presence and treat his followers there to wonderful, exclusive glimpses into his life.

When he was jamming backstage at a concert he made sure it was filmed, so his fans could catch some behind-the-scenes snatches of how life on the road was for him. On 4 August he uploaded a video showing him jamming with his guitar to the song 'Heartless' by rap legend Kanye West and the Drake song 'Successful'. With a claret-coloured T-shirt on and a huge white watch on his wrist he looks cool and, as ever, he sings and plays the guitar brilliantly.

The text sign-off on the video paid tribute to Mr West, 'This one's for you Kanye – Justin'. Little could Justin have known that with a few months he would be publicly defending another artist from what he felt was unfair treatment by Kanye West.

In the meantime, as his album release neared, what could Justin tell his army of fans about what to expect from it? 'It's gonna be a fun album,' he revealed on *MTV News*. 'It's a lot about love and teen love and what would be in my world.' However, this was not the only theme of the release, Justin added. 'There's a lot of stuff that's not just about love,' he continued. 'There's songs that teens can relate to, as far as parents not being together and divorce and just stuff that happens in everyday life. There's a lot of kids my age and their whole album is "Everything is perfect". Real life isn't perfect, so my album kind of portrays that. You just have to make the best of what you have. I'm looking forward to influencing others in a positive way.

'My message is you can do anything if you just put your mind to it. I grew up below the poverty line; I didn't have as much as other people did. I think it made me stronger as a person, it built my character. Now I have a 4.0 grade point average and I want to go to college and just become a better person.'

As ever, Justin and his team had a great marketing idea up their sleeves to help make his album a success. Their idea was to offer fans a chance to meet him – but, as in the children's classic *Charlie and the Chocolate Factory*, only if they found one of the golden tickets that would be inserted into some of his CD cases. Justin was excited to announce his very own golden ticket contest to his Twitter followers. 'IT'S TRUE!!' he wrote. 'There will be GOLDEN TICKETS in some of my albums . . . U find the right album you get a PRIVATE CONCERT for u and your friends!!!'

His next Tweet explained that the album was going to be released over two parts. 'The word is getting out 2day,' he wrote. 'MY WORLD is going to come out in 2 parts. Part 1 is Nov 17th and Part 2 will start Valentines week next year.' The anticipation for Part 1 was so intense that many fans could not even look ahead as far as Part 2! Justin confirmed that he had been working with a great team. 'I've been working with Tricky Stewart and The-Dream, I've worked with a bunch of other people,' he said. 'I worked with the Movement, the Clutch. A lot of good producers and stuff.'

Everything being said about the album sounded great, and so to the all-important question: what did the album itself actually sound like? It opened with the familiar sound of his debut single 'One Time'. It was the obvious track with which to start the album and as Justin chanted on it 'my world, is your world', he was reminding listeners of the title of the album itself. 'Favorite Girl' follows, and as that song finishes, track 3 begins with Justin whispering the word 'mafia' over a piano track.

Don't worry, this was not in reference to any sort of crime mob but rather the Midi Mafia production duo who had created the song alongside him. This was the first track on the album in which Justin had been involved in the writing. So it is no surprise that 'Down to Earth' is one of the more personal tracks on *My World*. As Justin told *Billboard* magazine, 'It's a ballad about the feelings I had when my parents split up and how I helped my family get through it. I think a lot of kids have had their parents split up, and they should know that it wasn't because of something they did. I hope people can relate to it.'

The lyrics – about fighting through hurt while going through a difficult period – are indeed ones that surely any human being can relate to. The lyrics are painful and heartbreaking as Justin sings about the hurt and confusion he is going through. The truth is that many young people go through exactly these feelings as they are growing up and dealing with what life throws at them. For Justin to put these challenging times into words and then set them to music explains why he is such an inspiration to the young. He understands better than anyone what it means to be young and he provides a soundtrack to those experiences.

However, much as his lyrics are sad and honest, there is always a note of positivity there too. Justin admits in 'Down to Earth' that it's not an easy situation to deal with, but he believes that if he sticks with those who love him, he can make it through the challenge. Some young fans were so moved by his combination of courage, strength and vulnerability in this song that they cried as they listened to it. Justin, it can be argued, is the voice of a generation.

The next song on the album is called 'Bigger'. Again, it had the Midi Mafia team involved in its creation, so once more Justin whispers the word 'mafia' as the song begins. However, this song could hardly be more different musically to the one that came before it. 'Bigger' is an uptempo tune with an air of happy defiance, in which Justin looks back to his earlier years and the bullies who made him unhappy and notes with joy that he is now bigger than them.

Some commentators noted that the lines about how he was a 'heartbreaker' and 'player' when he was younger sounded odd coming from one so young, but the fans were too busy dancing along to such a catchy pop track – three minutes and seventeen seconds of dancing joy!

The message of the song is to encourage his fans and listeners to set their sights high and aim for bigger goals. Hard to argue with that!

Next up is the happy and heart-warming song 'One Less Lonely Girl', which lifts the mood after the more serious and moving theme of 'Down to Earth'. Indeed, 'One Less Lonely Girl' is a song that resonates with Justin's young female fans.

'First Dance', the next track on the album, is a song Justin describes as, 'a slow, groovy song that people can dance to'. It begins with the voice of Justin's mentor Usher, but soon Justin's voice takes over as he sings sweetly about that rite of passage familiar to so many children, particularly in America: the first dance with a partner at a school prom!

He sings about how the first dance leads to the first kiss, in which he tastes the girl's lip gloss. He makes a nod to the Cinderella story by referring to 'glass slippers'. He wants to take the whole experience slowly because, after all, you only have a first time once in your life. As we saw, Justin's real first kiss at a prom was a little awkward – so he was singing from experience on that front!

The melody of the song is similar to one used by Justin's hero Michael Jackson, reminding quite a few listeners of Jackson's hit song 'You Are Not Alone'. For Justin, who grew up idolizing Jackson, this was a comparison he found very flattering. The final track of the album was 'Love Me', the single with the sampled chorus. As discussed before this is a contagious and enjoyable pop tune – so it ended a great album on a great note!

Or did it? For there were two secret bonus tracks for the fans to enjoy. The first, 'Common Denominator', is one of Justin's most sweet and heartfelt songs. He tells the girl of the song that the only thing he fears in life is no longer having her with him. He would, he vows sweetly, face a thousand years of pain. He brings in mathematical themes when he explains that he does not wish to ever return to being just one-half of an equation. The girl is, he explains, the common denominator of his life. At four minutes and two seconds, it is one of the longer songs on the album and many would argue it is the most heart-warming. It was almost enough to make maths lessons a little less painful! Either way, Justin surely knows how to press the buttons of his female fans and is quite the young charmer. The next bonus track was for Canadian fans only and was a French adaptation of 'One Less Lonely Girl'. These bonus tracks – two extra treats for Justin's devoted fans – were there to tide them over until the release of the second part of the album in 2010.

The reaction to the first part of *My World* was, in the main, very admiring. Many people thought it was the best pop album to hit the shelves in a long time. The influential *Rolling Stone* magazine might be aimed at readers much older than Justin's key fans, but it knows a good pop album when it hears one. It gave *My World* three out of five, and focused its praise on one song in particular, saying, 'But who could deny "First Dance", where Usher drops Justin at the prom so he and his Bieblette can get to "rockin' back and forth under the disco ball"?'

The main BBC website review said that the album would be enjoyed by many people, especially 'those of a similar age to the artist', and the review concluded on a happy, admiring note, describing Justin as 'a cheeky chap rightfully having the time of his young life'. The website's page aimed specifically at younger viewers was also impressed, 'The teen singing sensation has become a huge hit in loads of countries, and his latest offering won't disappoint . . . *My World* is a great album and it's hard to find anything wrong with it.'

Justin was particularly interested to hear what the newspapers in his native Canada had to say about the album. *The Toronto Star* newspaper wrote that, 'His album is chock full of catchy tunes that are destined to be played incessantly by Justin Bieber's 'tween base and that, thankfully, their parents will find tolerable.' The reviewer concluded: 'With an album that delivers on his promise, the only thing we could ask is more.'

Back in America, David Hiltbrand of the *Philadelphia Inquirer* was impressed with Justin's album too. '*My World* is a catchy, well-executed treat,' he wrote. 'Particularly the frisky romps about puppy love like "One Time". Sure, Bieber is less convincing on a break-up ballad such as "Back to Earth". But there's no denying that this baby-faced soul boy has talent. And he's cute. Let the young girls scream!'

They did indeed scream – and they're still screaming to this day!

Mikael Wood of the influential magazine *Entertainment Weekly* said, 'At fifteen, this pint-size Canadian crooner is still more than a decade younger than Usher and Justin Timberlake, both of whom offered the singer record deals based on his hit YouTube channel. (Usher won.) Not surprisingly, *My World* is long on sugary puppy-love ballads and dinky dance-pop confections; diabetics are advised to stay away. Bieber's better on "Love Me", where he riffs on the Cardigans' "Lovefool" atop a killer electro-glam groove. Here's hoping his swagger grows with age.'

On and on the praise came Justin's way. The reviewer for the website AllMusic was also impressed, writing that Justin 'more than gets by on his squeaky-clean charm and natural ability'. Perhaps the highest praise came from the mighty American newspaper *The New York Times*, which said that Justin's work is comparable with his boyhood hero Michael Jackson and that some of the songs on the album are 'are uncomplicatedly beautiful and earnest'. *Billboard* described Justin's vocals as being 'as boyish as they are disarmingly mature'. This contrast is similar to the winning combination of Justin's cheeky childish side with his wiser, older head.

So, there was plenty for Justin to be proud of as he leafed and clicked his way through the critics' verdicts. Around the time of the release of *My World* he did a lot of interviews to promote the album. Through these his fans gained new insights into what makes him tick as far as music goes, and in his life in general. When asked why he had chosen *My World* as the title of the album he said, 'Basically it was the only way I could really describe it. It's so many elements of my world.' Although his fan base is dominated by young people, especially young girls, Justin insisted that his album should appeal to other people too. 'I think older people can appreciate my music because I really show my heart when I sing, and it's not corny,' he said. 'I think I can grow as an artist and my fans will grow with me.'

Speaking of fans of different sizes, Justin sang 'Bigger' at the MTV Video Music Awards. Wearing a light brown jumper and blue jeans, Justin looked very cool and was in energetic mood. 'I think I'm ready,' he said just before the song kicked off. He performed brilliantly, flanked by a pair of dancers. Naturally, most of the girls watching screamed with excitement, and their screams could even be heard above the loud track blasting out of the speakers. Whenever Justin looked out into the audience many of them waved manically, hoping to grab a precious moment of his attention.

He also showed up on the German television show *The Dome*. Filmed in front of an audience many thousands strong, once again, Justin was almost deafened by the fans' screams as he performed 'One Time'. He was clearly singing live but also managed to dance well. Some pop stars find it hard to dance and sing live at the same time. They therefore sometimes choose to mime the vocals so they can concentrate on dancing, or sacrifice the dancing in favour of singing live. But Justin showed what a professional he is by combining both excellently.

As he ran around the large stage the girls nearest to him at any given point screamed with all the more excitement. This was Biebermania in action! 'I love you, guys,' the boy himself shouted when the song finished. 'You guys are so awesome – thank you so much!'

The presenter said 'Justin Bieber: "One Time", for the first time, at *The Dome*!' She told Justin how stunned she had been by the excitement he had generated. 'It's so amazing,' he agreed. Turning to the crowd he said, 'I love you guys so much.' He then waved to the ecstatic throng. It seemed that Europe loved him just as noisily as America and Canada did.

His quest for global domination was working so far.

As well as appearing on television shows, Justin also made several in-store appearances at big stores in America. These were good opportunities for his fans to see him in person. One of these events was held at the Nintendo World Store on the famous Rockerfeller Plaza in New York. It was supposed to be an intimate performance for just 300 guests, but it soon became something far bigger than that as thousands of fans turned up to see him. Some had come the day before and slept overnight at the venue, so keen were they to see Justin. Many had travelled for hours to be there. He wore a purple jumper over his white T-shirt and sat on a stool, performing a soulful, acoustic rendition of 'One Time'. Naturally, the girls who had been lucky enough to get into the store were going crazy.

After singing to them, Justin was keen to give something to the disappointed fans who had not been able to get into the store. There were thousands of them outside, so he leant out of a window and waved to them, blowing them kisses and making a 'heart' sign with his hands. It was a sweet and classy gesture from a boy who, though stunned by the extent of his fan base, is nonetheless always keen to treat them kindly and fairly – gestures that do *not* go unnoticed by them.

He was soon back at the Rockerfeller Plaza – but this time it was to appear on one of America's biggest ever television shows. *The Today Show* is one of the most important and talked-about programmes ever to grace American television. It was first broadcast back in the 1950s, the first morning television show to hit the airwaves, and quickly became a massively popular and influential programme, remaining so today. The world's biggest stars and politicians dream of the chance to appear on *The Today Show*; Justin was invited to appear twice in quick succession. So in October he was back at the Plaza to perform for the NBC show.

He trailed the performance four days beforehand when he spoke to the show to promote 'Read for the Record', a national campaign to promote reading and literacy among children. Speaking of his fame he described it as 'really amazing' and said he had never expected his life and career to turn out this way. 'I have an idea. I think that everybody, just come down, bring your books . . . and we're going to donate them to the organization.'

On the day of the actual performance it was a little bit chilly in New York, so Justin wore a black jacket and wrapped a grey scarf around his neck. After the DJ had warmed up the crowd Justin – who looked a little nervous – ran onto the stage and sang 'One Time'. The girls assembled there screamed and sang along with joy. 'Make some noise for Justin Bieber,' said the MC as the song ended, and the crowd duly did just that. This was not the end of his appearance on the hit show.

He returned later in the morning, to sit on a stool and perform an acoustic version of 'Favorite Girl'. Again, the fans were overjoyed. After the song finished they went mad, much to the amazement of the presenters, one of whom asked, 'How would you like to be that sort of sensation at that age?'

After this performance Justin jetted across America to appear on San Diego radio. Then it was on to Tennessee for yet more radio chats. What a glamorous lifestyle he was leading as he promoted his debut album! *The Today Show* presenter was right – Justin was a sensation!

Next up on his tour was an appearance on *The Next Star*, a Canadian reality television show. It was the night of the live finale, so the atmosphere was already electric. Then Justin took to the stage and the roof nearly lifted off the venue. Wearing his green jumper and claret T-shirt, he was also wearing a prominent crucifix. He sat onstage next to a co-guitarist and after some horseplay with the screaming crowd, the pair launched into an acoustic rendition of 'One Less Lonely Girl'. Here, the hysteria was almost frightening. Girls did not just sing along and scream and wave at Justin: they burst into tears too.

His second song on the night was 'One Time'. For this the guitars and stools were cleared away so he could perform the song to its normal backtrack. When he sang the chorus it was clear how packed the venue was with hardcore Justin fans – the audience's voices nearly drowned him out as they sang along with joy. 'Love Justin' said one of the banners in the audience – certainly seeming to speak for everyone present.

'Good job, buddy – great job!' said the presenter, joining Justin onstage after the song had ended. He then explained that they had lined up a surprise for Justin … and handed him a plaque to mark the milestone that 'One Time' had gone platinum. Justin accepted the plaque and held it up in victory. 'Thank you so much, thank you so much,' he said. He then leant down to give the rather short girl who had presented him with the plaque a hug. It was a very cute moment. 'Make sure to pick up Justin's album,' said the host. Like anyone needed reminding of that!

On its release, *My World* sold well and this was due in part to the many promotional ideas Justin and his team used. Having set a competition requiring fans to create videos that imaginatively promoted the song 'One Time', Justin was the focus point of a similar contest when *My World* was released. When he planned a small private show for I Heart Radio, the station asked fans to upload videos of themselves singing 'One Time', yet again making the fans feel as if they were a real part of Justin's story.

His next competition was even cooler – it saw him donate a signed T-shirt to the leading animal welfare group PETA (People for the Ethical Treatment of Animals). 'My Dad and I used to go and hang out … just go and visit the different animals and stuff,' said Justin of his interest in animal welfare. 'It's really important that people adopt. I really encourage going out to an animal shelter or a place where you can get a dog that has been abandoned or doesn't have a home.' He also posed for a PETA poster, on which ran the slogan, 'My World Includes Compassion for Animals. Yours Should Too'.

As Justin ran the gauntlet of the promotional trail, he learned fast how to promote himself and his music effectively. He knew that it was important to get the message across about what his latest and forthcoming releases were. This did not just make his management and record company happy, it was also helpful for his fans: they wanted to know what was going on in his world and when they would next get the chance to buy something Justin-related.

For instance, in one interview on Fox television's *All Access* show, Justin reeled off the dates for his releases – and his interviewer was clearly impressed. 'Fifteen and he's plugging like an animal here,' said the interviewer, while Justin smiled proudly in agreement. 'It's like, he's got all the dates and everything going on here!' Turning to Justin he said, 'You're doing a fine job!'

The Fox interview was a very personal one and gave Justin's fans the chance to learn more about the boy behind the music. 'Yeah, I sing a lot about love,' Justin told the interviewer, who then asked him what a boy his age could know about love. 'Erm, I think it feels good,' said Justin with a nervous giggle. 'I mean, I'm not an expert about love, or anything. I'm still learning, I'm still trying to get the process . . .' The interviewer suggested jokingly that maybe Justin needed 'about a year and a half' to master the concept of love. He agreed with this. 'I'm single and ready to mingle,' he added. He was then asked about the ages of his past girlfriends. 'Er, the oldest is, like, sixteen and a half,' replied Justin. 'Older woman!' said the interviewer with a smile. 'I'll go out with anyone I fall in love with, I guess,' said Justin. 'And you just know that from some feeling inside?' asked the interviewer. 'Yeah,' said Justin. He was also asked if he had ever cried over a girl. 'No, not yet,' said Justin. 'I haven't really dated that many girls, I'm just trying to get this whole love thing down.'

Justin also talked about his schooling, explaining that despite being famous and successful he was still learning, completing much of his schooling via online classes. In another chat he expanded on his post-fame learning. 'I have a tutor,' he said. 'I want to go to college. As Asher Roth says, I think college would be a blast.' Asked what subject he might choose to study at college he gave a hint at what it might be, 'I'm good at English,' he said. 'I like to write.' Having been involved in the writing of two songs featured on *My World*, fans can expect more songwriting from Justin in the future.

He has impressed many interviewers with his mature and poised handling of their questions. When examiner.com asked him about other celebrities during an interview he calmly pointed out that they kept returning to the theme, saying: 'You guys are asking me about a lot of celebs'. He is not one to be easily pushed into making unwise but headline-grabbing remarks.

An interview on ABC television's *Good Morning America* became one of the most meaningful television packages around the release of the album. 'I still listen to the radio,' he said, when asked about how fame had changed him, 'but I used to listen to it just to hear other people. It's crazy – now I listen to the radio and I hear myself!' He reflected on his performances at the Stratford Star with a hint of embarrassment. 'I was a loser,' he said, which was a little harsh on himself!

Usher was then shown and he explained that Justin already had a huge online following before he even discovered him. 'It was truly his talent. Truly his ability on the spot to produce that magic,' said Usher of Justin. As for Justin himself, he tried to sum up how he was dealing with the ever-building hysteria around him. 'It still feels like a dream,' he explained. 'Like, I'm starting to realize that this is crazy.'

His mother then joined the interview to explain how she was keeping an eye on Justin amid the craziness. 'I feel like if there's too much pressure on him then we scale back and we cancel some things and stuff like that. We're just taking it one day at a time, and try and get proper rest.' It was reassuring to be reminded that the person closest to

Justin was concerned more about his personal welfare than his professional career.

Usher was also quizzed about how carefully Justin was being treated. 'How do you make sure he doesn't burn out?' Usher was asked. 'There's no time for that, there's no time for him burning out right now,' he replied.

Soon after, in another interview on CNN, he repeated again how shocked he was by his rise to fame. 'It caught me way off guard, it's just been an amazing process,' Justin said. Not that he was complaining, 'Like I always tell people: what fifteen-year-old wouldn't want screaming girls waiting for him all the time?' He also confirmed that he and Usher were 'very close'.

And Justin's advice to budding Biebers? 'Just follow your dream – you can do anything you set your mind to. That's basically it!'

Back in Canada, Justin was in just as much demand. He spoke to the leading Canadian television network CTV about his life and how he had risen from his humble childhood in Canada to become a growing global star.

He was clearly happy with his lot and seemed to be keeping calm amid the earthquake of excitement his pop career was generating. 'I love being on stage,' he said. 'I love to be able to perform for my fans. I like to get to see their smile and being able to hear their screaming because I'm doing something that they want. I really love to perform.'

He also touched on the future. 'Five years down the road, I see myself furthering my career, maybe win a Grammy.' So there is clearly no shortage of ambition on Justin's part. Who would doubt that he will go on to achieve much more success?

True to form, he uploaded a short video to his YouTube channel to thank the fans for the success he had enjoyed so far. 'So, as you guys all know, I'm from a little town in Stratford, Ontario, Canada. A town of 30,000 people. I never dreamed this day would come. My album is in stores and I'm just so excited. You guys made my dreams come true. Like I said, I never thought this would happen so thank you guys so much. I really appreciate it.'

As Scooter Braun explained, Justin's interaction with fans online – particularly via the Twitter site – was an important thing. 'If I see he's not Twittering, I tell him, "Get on your Twitter". Because it's how his fans relate to him. They made him, you know?

'The moment he disappears from them, they feel like they've lost that kid from YouTube that invited them into his living room.' As for Justin, he enjoys managing his own image and his instant interaction with fans. 'I keep it all on here, it's all on my iPhone,' he said. 'I enjoy updating my status. Tweets and stuff.'

Meantime, in the aftermath of these two prestigious interview slots, Justin received another boost in the shape of a series of honours and other pieces of positive news. First, he was invited to make his second appearance in a fortnight on the *Ellen DeGeneres Show*. Then *My World* hit the Number 1 spot in Canada, and sales of the album made him the highest-selling debut artist of 2009 at that point. (He was overtaken at the end of the year by *Britain's Got Talent* sensation Susan Boyle.) As all this was happening he passed 100 million views on his YouTube account.

Just two years before all this, Justin had been sitting outside the theatre in Stratford, busking with his guitar and slowly earning enough money to take his mother on holiday. Everything was happening so quickly it was hard for Justin to draw breath – and there wasn't the slightest chance of him having a rest any time soon either.

With a whole new set of commitments lined up, and an ever-swelling fan base of fanatical followers on the horizon, Justin had only begun to understand what it means to be a famous pop legend.

People were widely predicting that there was more, much more, to come for Justin. Nick Cannon – who had starred on a YouTube video with Justin as his mainstream fame first started taking off – predicted the fifteen-year-old Justin would become a global sensation imminently.

'Justin Bieber's definitely about to take the world by storm if he hasn't already,' Cannon explained. 'He's filling a void that hasn't been filled since the Backstreet Boys and 'N Sync and all of that stuff.' Celebrity blogger Perez Hilton – on whose website Justin had launched one of his promotional videos and who he had met for a special recorded performance a few months earlier – was also convinced that Biebermania was only going to get more intense.

'He's already become this phenomenon and it's only gonna get bigger and bigger and bigger,' said Hilton.

And he was absolutely right . . .

7

Biebermania

We have already seen how Justin's path first crossed with that of country pop singer Taylor Swift. His video for 'One Less Lonely Girl' was directed by the man who had directed a Taylor Swift video. Then Swift used a Justin song as the soundtrack to her tour diary video, and he responded with an acoustic version of 'Favorite Girl'. However, in 2009, his connection with Swift became a whole lot more exciting when he was asked to introduce her at the MTV Video Music Awards (VMAS) night.

A very important night in the entertainment industry calendar, the VMAS was first held in 1984 as MTV began to establish itself as the home of the music industry video. Since then, the televised event has been held in several American locations, including New York City, Los Angeles, Miami and Las Vegas. It has seen many memorable moments including eye-catching performances from Madonna and Michael Jackson in the 1980s, and more recently the likes of Britney Spears and the Backstreet Boys have made sure the VMAS are never far from the headlines.

In 2009, the VMAS was to prove to be no ordinary awards night. Controversial British comedian Russell Brand hosted the event and brought an offbeat sense of humour to the proceedings. The previous year Brand had sparked a great deal of controversy, but at the VMAS in New York in 2009 he was upstaged in terms of controversy by one of the music artists present at the ceremony.

When Taylor Swift won the award for the Best Female Video for her song 'You Belong to Me', she was initially delighted. As she began her acceptance speech she was breathless with excitement. 'I always wondered what it would be like to maybe win one of these someday, but never actually thought it would happen,' she said.

However, there was then a rude interruption as rap star Kanye West jumped onto the stage and took the microphone from Taylor.

West – who had been photographed swigging alcohol as he arrived at the event – was determined to have his say. 'Yo Taylor,' he said, as she and the audience looked on stunned. 'I'm really happy for you, I'm going to let you finish, but Beyoncé had one of the best videos of all time.'

Swift was too stunned to continue her speech properly. As for West, he was ejected from the ceremony shortly afterwards. When Beyoncé won a separate award later in the evening she called Swift to the stage to make up with a hug.

West later apologized on his blog. 'I'm sooooo sorry to Taylor Swift and her fans and her mom. I'm in the wrong for going on stage and taking away from her moment. Beyoncé's video was the best of this decade ... I'm sorry to my fans if

I let you guys down … I'm sorry to my friends at MTV . . . I will apologize to Taylor.'

Despite this, West was widely criticized, with even President Barack Obama expressing his disapproval of West's behaviour. However, one person had been quick to comfort Swift even before either Beyoncé or West did: step forward Justin Bieber! Straight after West's interruption, Justin took to the stage to prepare to present Swift's live performance. With actor and singer Miranda Cosgrove alongside him, he said, 'First off, I'd just like to say, give it up for Taylor Swift – she deserved that award!' Justin was probably the youngest person present at the awards but it was he who took the most mature – and thoughtful – approach on the night. The crowd cheered his kind and conciliatory words for the upset Swift.

Later in the evening Taylor herself was quick to thank Justin for his kindness, as he explained to *Billboard*. 'After I presented, Taylor Swift thanked me for saying that she deserved to win her award. She said "Thanks for sticking up for me, lil' bro'" and I was like "Yeah, I've got your back."'

He was also asked how he felt taking on such a huge role as presenting another artist live onstage at a glamorous awards ceremony. After all it was not just a huge audience, it was a huge audience packed with stars. 'I wasn't nervous at all,' said Justin. 'I never get nervous. I don't think any performer really does.'

It had been quite a rollercoaster evening for Justin. He had met and witnessed a performance from Beyoncé, much to his excitement. 'It was crazy, I was like in love with her,' he said. 'I was shaking in my boots.' On a more sombre note, the tributes paid on the evening to Michael Jackson, who had died just two months earlier, were very moving for Justin. Having grown up loving and being influenced by Jackson's music, he had hoped at some point to stand alongside Jackson at a big musical event, but here he was, watching tributes to his late hero.

Michael Jackson's death in 2009 had shocked the world. His passing made many people remember that, for all the strange aspects of his life, Jackson was an extraordinary pop talent. Justin was as shaken up as everyone else and had himself paid his own tribute to Jackson on his YouTube channel the previous month.

While he was on the road promoting his music Justin bumped into a busker on the street. They got chatting and Justin was reminded of his own time busking, back in Stratford. He asked the busker, who was playing a cello, to give him a backing track so he could sing the legendary Michael Jackson song 'Billie Jean'. Justin then moonwalked, in homage to the dance made famous by Jackson.

The resulting video was posted on Justin's YouTube channel, complete with the text 'RIP Michael'. It was a sweet way for Justin to show his respect to his hero, who had died at the age of fifty. Given how early Justin began his pop career, there have been comparisons made between himself and Michael Jackson. Everyone hopes that Justin will remain the wholesome and sensible character he is, even as his fame continues to soar.

This sort of activity on YouTube showed that Justin planned to continue using his kidrauhl channel. He had been asked by *Billboard* whether he intended to carry on using online methods. 'Oh, definitely. I think the Internet is the best way to reach your fans. A couple of years back, artists didn't have that tool, so why not use it now? I'm also on Facebook, and my fans got together and sent me a "Get Well" card on Twitter when I was sick the other day. That was really cool. For now, I'm too worried about getting too close to the fans. I don't share much personal information.'

When he did share any information it was snapped up by the fans. For instance, when he had visited London in the summer of 2009 just one Tweet announcing where he was instantly drew hundreds of fans to the building! They screamed for Justin and he duly obliged their wishes by taking his guitar to the street outside and singing 'One Time' for them.

They sang along and screamed at him – it seems Bieber fans have plenty in common whichever country they are in. Justin then patiently signed autographs for them. Some wanted posters signed, others opted to have their clothing or even electrical equipment scrawled on by their hero. The one thing they all had in common was that they left him with a huge smile on their faces.

In November he visited the rap artist Diddy. Born Sean Combs, Diddy has had an illustrious career that included him producing some of Usher's material. It was through this connection that Justin got to spend time with Diddy. On a video shot from the time they spent together Diddy promised to give Justin a flash car 'as soon as you turn sixteen'. He showed him the car, a silver sports model, and very impressed Justin was. Justin cheekily suggested that even though he was only fifteen maybe Diddy might let him have a drive already. 'No, slow down, slow down Just,' said Diddy. 'When you're sixteen, you're good to go. Then, when you're eighteen – you get the house!' Diddy then turned to the camera and joked around more.

'I have been given custody of him,' he said, nodding to Justin. 'He's signed to Usher, but I had legal guardianship of Usher when he did his first album. I don't have legal custody of [Justin] but for the next forty-eight hours he's with me.' Justin ended the video by jokingly suggesting they 'go and get some girls'. Rough and ready videos like this one are brilliant ways for Justin to connect with his fans, and judging by the hits each video receives, the fans just love them.

He continued to give the fans chances to see him in person, too. In November he played at Toronto's Kool Haus club. A reviewer who saw the show wrote that Justin had 'all the stage swagger and moxie Usher and Timberlake have honed over the years . . . but it was his non-choreographed efforts that resonated the most'. The following month Justin was even busier with live shows. He appeared at the Twin Cities concert in St Paul. As Christmas approached he also appeared at a Jingle Ball in Camden, New Jersey, bringing plenty of festive cheer to his excitable fans. There was another Jingle Ball in Boston the following day and then a third a few days later. The final Jingle Ball was on 20 December in Tulsa, Oklahoma. Joining Justin on the bill were pop-punk band Bowling For Soup and solo artist Priscilla Renea.

These were successful and happy events. Sure, the reaction Justin prompted was often bordering on the hysterical, but they passed off without any serious incident. But unfortunately this wasn't always to be the case: life was about to get a lot more complicated for Justin and his management as they were confronted by the realities of fan mania.

In November 2009 Justin was due to make an official appearance at the Roosevelt Field Mall in the Garden City neighbourhood of Long Island, New York. It should have been a relatively simple engagement to fulfil.

He was due to sign copies of his new album at the clothing store Justice. However, the day was going to go badly wrong. That morning, Justin let his fans know where he was going to be. At 9.08 a.m. he Tweeted 'Going to be at Roosevelt Field Mall in Long Island, NY today signing MY WORLD at 4 p.m. See everyone there.'

Just before midday Justin again updated his Twitter account and wrote: 'On my way to Roosevelt Field Mall in Long Island, NY to sign and meet fans!! im pumped. see u there.' Everybody expected Justin's appearance to draw a large and excitable crowd to the mall. But it soon became clear that the crowd was going to be unmanageable.

An estimated 3,000 fans swarmed to the shopping mall to meet their hero. Some of them had arrived before dawn in the hope of gaining a special viewpoint. Still, few could have guessed just how badly wrong things would go.

Before long the numbers had swelled far beyond 3,000, and by the time of the scheduled event according to some estimates the crowd was nearer to 10,000 strong. Around thirty-five police officers had been sent in to try and control the growing frenzy.

Eyewitnesses later explained the scenes that they encountered. 'People started screaming, "Justin!" And they ran forward and the ropes collapsed,' a thirteen-year-old girl who was caught up in the mayhem told reporters. 'There were thousands of people pushing, shoving, crying,' added Lisa Slawinski, a mother who had brought her daughter to see Justin.

Police quickly grew genuinely concerned about the situation. As the chaos got worse, at 1.30 p.m. Justin Tweeted: 'They are not allowing me to come into the mall. if you dont leave I and my fans will be arrested as the police just told us.' The appearance was cancelled, but that was not the end of the matter, for the fallout was serious. Five of Justin's fans were taken to hospital. The police claimed that their request for Justin's management to announce via Twitter that the event was cancelled was not responded to quickly enough, also adding that the whole event had been a 'prescription for disorder'.

The press was quick to report the story. One newspaper used the headline 'Fandemonium'. Justin was extremely upset by what had happened. He wrote on Twitter: 'wow. this upsets me. the mall should of had proper security. They wouldnt let me in! Gotta make this right 4 the fans'.

Justin's label, Island Records, told the *New York Daily News*: 'Over 10,000 screaming fans showed up and the police and fire marshal concluded it was an unsafe environment and prohibited the event from taking place.' Justin's fans were left shaken and heartbroken as well. 'I feel like crying right now; we love him,' said one fourteen-year-old fan.

Justin and Pattie were very keen to let people know that they backed Braun and felt he had done nothing wrong whatsoever. 'My mother and I are 100 per cent behind my manager,' Bieber wrote in a statement. 'He is someone of high moral character and principle. The decisions he made that day were to protect the safety of myself and my fans, and I am very thankful to have someone in my life who watches over me the way Scooter does.'

He later explained on the radio show of Los Angeles DJ Ryan Seacrest what had happened from his perspective. 'I wanna see my fans. I don't wanna look like a jerk, like a no-show . . . I wanna say hi to my fans, but when I got there the police threatened to put me in cuffs and take me and my mum to the penitentiary,' he said. 'They were threatening to put me in jail. They were like, "If you don't pull off right now, we're gonna arrest you and your mother." We're not trying to get deported – me and my mum are Canadian. We were just like, "Whatever." So we pulled off, went away and it turns out the cops were holding another person . . . the vice-president of the label. They had him and were like, "If Justin doesn't Twitter for everyone to go home, then we're gonna send you to jail." My phone was dead; I had no clue what was going on.' Sadly, this was not to be the last time that an appearance by Justin sparked chaotic and frightening scenes.

Meanwhile, after some of his fans had been taken to hospital as a result of the Long Island mall chaos, it was Justin himself who was next to be rushed through the doors of a hospital after injuring himself onstage. It was while he was in London that the disaster struck, and the way he handled it was a true testament to his personal strength of character and his professional dedication.

The trip to England came about because his fellow teen sensation and good friend Taylor Swift was playing two dates in England in November. Her *Fearless* album was proving a big hit around the world and she had been touring with *American Idol* star Kellie Pickler and country music group Gloriana as her support acts. These two acts would each perform to warm up the crowd at Swift's concerts, before the star of the evening took to the stage. However, when it came to her two UK dates, due to other commitments both these acts were unable to travel with Swift. So who did she turn to? Justin! He was an obvious choice: popular, a great performer and also a friend. 'She's even nicer in real life,' Justin had told examiner.com. 'She is the best and you should all support her.' It seemed a dream arrangement for both Swift and Justin. What could possibly go wrong?

The last thing Justin expected was that he would injure himself while performing at Swift's Wembley Arena show. Performing in front of an 11,000-strong audience, as ever, Justin was putting on a show of sheer star quality. All was going swimmingly as he began his final song of the evening.

The audience was lapping up every moment and singing along with him as he sang 'One Time'. Then – disaster struck! He tripped during his performance and felt an immediate pain in one of his ankles. As Justin later explained on his Twitter feed: 'In the last song ONE TIME I tripped over something on stage coming down the ramp and felt my ankle roll in a very bad way.' He later posted the true, horrible extent of his injury: 'Turns out I fractured my foot'.

What was amazing about the incident was that the fracture didn't stop him from completing his performance.

For him, the show must go on and he stayed onstage to finish the song. He was rushed straight to hospital after the show and was in a cast for around four weeks. Back onstage the following evening he was ready to fulfil the Manchester date, even though his leg was in a cast.

He even found time to joke with Swift. 'Taylor told me to break a leg last night so I tried,' he joked. 'I couldn't break a leg but I broke a foot for you.' To which Swift replied: 'It's kind of like a figurative statement. I meant "good luck, it's so good to have you!" You know, "break a leg".' Justin pointed to his leg, and said: 'I mean, I just wanted to do what you told me. So . . . sorry.'

He added that he was often asked in interviews what his most embarrassing moment was, 'and I never have an answer. Now I'm going to answer: "The time I broke my foot on stage".' His final word on the incident was via his Twitter feed: 'Taylor, you know it was your fault . . . lol,' he joked.

He had shown enormous courage and maturity by continuing his final song, despite the pain, and by bouncing straight back onto the stage the following night. Well, perhaps more 'hobbling' than bouncing, but the fact Justin was there at all showed how seriously he takes his professional commitments and how much his fans mean to him.

He knew that although it was a Taylor Swift headlining tour, many of those who were showing up in Manchester were also very excited to see him. So he was not about to let them down. Besides, Justin loves the thrill of performing live.

He dreamed of doing his own tour one day. The

closest he had come was a short 'mini-tour' around several Canadian cities a few weeks earlier to meet the fans. All the same, Justin loved the excitement of 'life on the road' moving from city to city.

The mini-tour came about after an offer from clothing brand Urban Behavior. Founded in the late 1980s Urban Behavior manufactures and sells cool clothes for guys and girls – just the sort of company who were keen to be associated with a cool act like Justin! They booked Justin to tour Canadian cities, putting in appearances at their stores at each stop.

He began at Vancouver on 1 November and then moved in subsequent days to Edmonton, Montreal, London (the Canadian London) and then Toronto. At each store, Justin met fans who were able to get an Urban Behavior T-shirt signed by their hero.

He was excited about all these appearances but, much to his and his fans' disappointment, he fell ill in the days leading up to the tour and was unable to fulfil the appearance at the Vancouver store.

To help ease the disappointment of his Vancouver fan base the Urban Behavior staff gave them discounts for the day and also provided a 'Get Well Soon' card that fans could sign. It was then sent on to Justin, to help cheer him up.

It certainly seemed to do the trick for he arrived for all

the other dates, and described the Montreal appearance as 'amazing' on his Twitter feed. 'Thanks to everyone who came out,' he wrote. 'I was surprised.' When he arrived in Toronto he gave all the fans who came a magical experience they will never forget. Straight after the store appearance he went to the city's Kool Haus venue to perform live to an audience of screaming girls!

Wearing a dark denim jacket and a back-to-front baseball cap, he looked amazing. As the audience screamed its delight he sang 'Bigger', dancing around as he did so. When he sang 'One Less Lonely Girl' he invited one fan to sit on the stage with him. He took his baseball cap off and put it on her head. Later in the show he touched the hands of the girls in the front row of the audience, prompting ever-louder screams.

He took the tempo down a bit with an acoustic performance of 'Favorite Girl'. The girls – all of whom wanted to be his favourite – sang along loudly, loving the moment of creative unity this offered them with their favourite boy. The dancers rejoined him for 'One Time', by which time the crowd was in seventh heaven!

'Make some noise for Justin Bieber!' said the MC at the end of the performance. These were hardly words that needed to be said – the girls were already virtually lifting the roof off the venue with their screams. Justin left the stage as the audience shouted in unison 'We love you, Justin!'

He then came back for an encore and spoke of his dream coming true. 'This has been like a cool rollercoaster ride. Thanks to awesome crowds like you guys,' he told them. Introducing the final song of the night he said, 'I'm going to need your help on this.' He then sang an *a capella* version of 'With You'. As he sang it, he might have considered how far he had come since first singing this Chris Brown song on his YouTube channel – and what an amazing turn his life had taken as a result of uploading home-made videos to the Internet.

Another consequence of Justin's fractured foot was that it put paid to a planned 'dance-off' he was hoping to have with Gabe Saporta, the lead singer and bassist from US rock band Cobra Starship. Appearing at the Jingle Ball in Sacramento, Saporta said that due to Justin's injury 'I win by default'. Well, Justin had a few things to say about that – and he arrived onstage to say them! 'All right, so what's going to go down is since I can't really dance for you I'm going to have to play an epic drum solo for you.'

Playing along with the pretend hostility, Saporta retorted 'You can't do that! Go back to Canada, kid!' But there was no stopping Justin, he sat at the drum kit and played a great solo. 'Thanks for showing me up, Justin,' said Saporta. 'I just got smoked by a kid half my size,' he added. 'I should just go home right now, right?'

It had all been good fun and Justin wrote about the evening on his YouTube channel page the following day. 'Playing the drums and using a broken foot on the pedal isnt easy so i dont know how "epic" this solo was but it was worth it,' he said. 'Gabe is the man and everyone in Cobra Starship are great people and we all had a lot of fun. Thanks to Sacramento for being such a great crowd.'

Whether it was performing in Manchester or drumming in Sacramento, there really was no holding Justin back. He had picked up the injury during a tour named Fearless – and he lived up to that theme in the way he carried on with his commitments. No one could call him a 'diva'.

He had tasted fame and loved it, but he wasn't going to let it go to his head. Divas have a talent for forgetting where they came from and losing sight of the fact that underneath their fame they are just the same as every other person. Justin has shown none of this behaviour. He is so full of enthusiasm and wholesome good character that he is unlikely to ever fall into the diva trap.

He had faced a few unhappy moments of late what with that injury and the cancelled event in the Long Island mall. But Justin was about to have a moment of sheer joy and pride – he was going to sing for Barack Obama, the President of the United States of America!

It was a very proud day for Pattie as she and her famous son flew to Washington DC to prepare for the big performance. They could hardly believe what they were travelling to the American capital to do.

The day before the show itself Justin took part in the rehearsals at the National Building Museum in Washington. Although this building doesn't quite have the prestige of the White House, it is nonetheless a stunning monument. As he practised his song, Justin surprised some of those watching when he took his phone out of his pocket and began clicking away on it. Surely Justin was not sending a text message while rehearsing a performance for the President of the United States of America? No, he was not. As he explained later, he was checking the lyrics for the song he was going to perform, 'Someday at Christmas' by Stevie Wonder. After all, he wanted to be word perfect for the big day!

Backstage, Scooter Braun told Justin that, as well as his solo performance of 'Someday at Christmas', he would also be required to join the entire ensemble onstage for a finale group performance of 'Hark! The Herald Angels Sing'. This was news to Justin.

'You know that one, right?' checked Braun. Justin shook his head. What to do? His manager had a suggestion. 'Just put the mike up to your mouth real close,' Braun suggested. 'Nobody will be able to see.' But Justin, he had another idea. 'I know "Deck the Halls",' he said, then sang beautifully, 'Deck the halls with poison ivy, fa-la-la-la-la ...' Confident and cheeky stuff, as we have come to expect from Justin. But he was honest enough to admit he was feeling a touch anxious too. And considering his audience, who wouldn't be?

On the night of the show Justin waited nervously while the other performers sang. Neil Diamond was the first to perform. The legendary star sang 'Joy to the World' and 'Winter Wonderland'. Then Mary J. Blige performed 'The Christmas Song (Chestnuts Roasting on an Open Fire)', after which Usher sang 'Have Yourself a Merry Little Christmas'.

Justin felt the butterflies in his stomach as the host introduced him. 'There's no Christmas without presents – really someone should have told my grandmother!' joked the host. 'And we have one for you tonight, Mr President and Mrs Obama. In the glory days of Motown an artist captured the attention of the world with this song which he turned into a classic. "Someday at Christmas" not only helped launch the career of one of your favourites, Stevie Wonder, but it has done the same via YouTube for our next artist tonight. Like you, Mr President, this young man has many fans trying to shake his hand without permission. Ladies and gentlemen, pop music's current sensation – Justin Bieber!' Justin then appeared on the stage to sing.

His nerves were clear, as he wrote on his YouTube channel afterwards. 'It was an incredible honor and I was really nervous. You can tell by my hands, I didn't know what to do with them . . . But what I am getting at is that all this has happened thanks to YouTube videos and fans like you. You have all changed my life forever and continue to change it with your support every day. I am extremely grateful and I hope you enjoy this "vid" and know that I wish you all a merry christmas and a great holiday season. Thank you again and best wishes to you and your family.'

Despite his nerves Justin sang brilliantly, with the choir alongside him. With a shirt and tie covered with a smart jumper, he certainly looked different to his usual 'street' image, but that was only appropriate for such an occasion. The audience applauded enthusiastically at the end of Justin's song. He waved to them and said: 'Thank you very much.'

As the end of the concert approached, President Obama addressed all who were present. During this talk he mispronounced Justin's surname. 'Thank you to all the incredible performers ... Rob Thomas, Usher and Justin Bye-ber ... BEE-ber!' The audience had a good laugh, but Obama quickly recovered from his mistake by jokingly saying of Justin: 'He was just discovered.'

The President continued to present the final song. 'This season we celebrate that sacred moment, the birth of a child, the message of love preached to the world,' he said, with First Lady Michelle Obama at his side. 'More than 2,000 years later, that spirit still inspires us.' Then they remained on the stage to join with the choir in a rendition of 'Hark! The Herald Angels Sing'.

What an honour and joy for Justin to have been part of this extraordinary evening. It was the culmination of an amazing seventy-two hours for him in which he made five separate performances in different parts of America. But performing for the President and First Lady was so special – professional honours do not get much bigger than that.

He had another proud moment in February 2010 when he was asked to take part in a charity single. More than eighty top pop stars helped record the song for the victims of the earthquake in Haiti. The chosen song was 'We Are the World', which had first been recorded twenty-five years earlier in aid of famine relief. In the original version the legendary Lionel Richie sang the opening line. This time the same line was sung by Justin. 'The experience was out of this world,' he said afterwards.

In the meantime, Justin had also begun his acting career. He appeared on the show *True Jackson, VP*, an American light comedy drama about the fashion industry. It is shown on the Nickelodeon channel and stars Keke Palmer.

On the day he began filming his appearance, Justin Tweeted: 'On the set of the show "True Jackson" in LA. Keke is really cool.' As for Keke, she wrote on her MySpace blog: 'I had a great time on set with Justin Bieber. He is so very talented and really sweet I know he will go very far in his career! He will be a guest star on an upcoming episode, I will keep y'all posted, but I am sure that Nickelodeon will show promo commercials way before informing you guys when this episode will air, it's gonna be a special one you don't want to miss!'

Justin also made a cameo appearance in an episode of the MTV drama *Silent Library* and in the movie *School Gyrls*.

In January 2010 he released another single, 'Baby'. Justin was involved in the writing and the song has a truly catchy chorus. The recording includes a rap from hip-hop star

Ludacris. '[Ludacris and I] both live in Atlanta,' explained Justin when asked how the collaboration came about. 'I met him a year prior to this and we figured it was a perfect collaboration for him, so we invited him out to do it.'

Ludacris needed little encouragement. 'As soon as I heard it I knew it was a hit, I just had to figure out how I could get on a record with a fifteen-year-old,' he said. 'So I sat there and said, "Let me reminisce on the past," and that's basically how I stepped on the record. And I guarantee you, mark my word, that's going to be one of the biggest songs of the year.'

The critics were impressed. Bill Lamb of About.com called it, 'the best vehicle yet for Justin Bieber's sweet soulful voice, and its chart achievements should ultimately reflect that fact'. Melanie Bertoldi of *Billboard* also predicted that the song would be a big hit in the charts. 'The mid-tempo number's undeniably contagious chorus should keep Bieber's tween fan base satisfied, and Ludacris's brief cameo adds a welcome urban twist. The match-up adds a layer of maturity to Bieber's repertoire and should further solidify his growing presence on the charts.'

It was indeed a hit, reaching the Top 5 in America, Canada and the UK. It was also a Top 10 hit in other countries, including France, New Zealand and Ireland. Justin was happy to have Ludacris's rapping on the track but he said he had no plans to try that type of vocals himself. 'No, not at all. Nope.'

The video for the single was shot in Los Angeles, and Justin explained the basic plot of the film. 'It starts off, I really like this girl, but we didn't [get] along; we couldn't be together,' he said. 'Basically I want her back and [I'm] kind of going through the whole thing. I'm chasing her around, trying to get her, and she's kind of playing hard to get, but I'm persistent. I keep going.' He compared the video to the one made by Michael Jackson for the single 'The Way You Make Me Feel'.

Just as his part in the video showed him persisting and charming his way towards a goal, so was Justin persistent in the real world. This in part explains the huge success he has enjoyed. But as we have seen, success comes with lows as well as highs.

Justin seems to spark hysteria wherever he goes, and in March 2010 there was an upsetting reminder of the scenes at Long Island when he flew to Philadelphia. He had been interviewed on a local radio station and while he was in the studio hundreds of excited fans surrounded the exit in the hope of a glimpse of him.

Despite all efforts to keep the situation under control, when Justin appeared there was chaos as the fans surged around him. Reports suggested some had grabbed at Justin and pulled his hair. Other people present said that Justin handled the frightening situation with grace and maturity.

Mindful of this growing peril during his public appearances, Justin sometimes decided to make personal sacrifices in order to keep a lid on safety. He had a party at the Lucky Strike bowling alley in New York in March, but left after being advised that the mob of fans descending on the venue could cause panic and injury. 'He wanted to stay and bowl, but his security guys didn't want to take any chances,' a spokesperson told the *New York Post*. Justin and his entourage quietly slipped away to the city's famous Eldridge Hotel, where they ordered burgers and fries all round.

Ever the caring gentlemen, when Justin saw that many of his party had leftovers on their plates, he decided they would drop the food off at a shelter for homeless people. Thanks to some sensible decisions, Justin and his team had prevented a possible disaster – and then gone on to turn the situation into a way of helping people less fortunate than themselves.

However, with his fame and the demands that put upon him, it was not long before Justin was once again put in a testing situation. This safety issue came when Justin was due to give a short early morning concert in Sydney, Australia.

The event was scheduled to take place at the city's famous harbour, starting at 7.40 a.m., but fans began arriving in the area the previous evening. Then a rumour circulated that Justin had arrived early, which caused an extra surge in numbers at around 2 a.m. The crowd went on growing and growing.

Over the following hours there were reports that some fans were crushed or trampled upon as they waited for Justin to appear. Some reports also said that a few of the barriers had been broken and that at least ten fans fainted in the resulting crush. One fan was taken to hospital with a fractured kneecap. 'There are a large number of kids down there without any parents there at all. And I would just question that,' said one police officer observing the scene.

Fearful of a real tragedy occurring, police ruled that the concert must be cancelled. 'Police have called off a planned concert this morning after several children required treatment for injuries received in the crowd crush,' said their statement. 'Police at the event were concerned for the four thousand excited people already in attendance, with many more anticipated to arrive prior to the start of the performance. Police have urged people to avoid the area to prevent further crowding and the possibility of associated injuries.'

When Justin woke up that morning he was surprised and disappointed to be told of the cancellation, though he always supports any step taken to keep his fans safe. When the concert's cancellation was announced, angry fans marched across the city and the police had their work cut out to control them.

As he had been after the Long Island event, Justin was very upset. He knew there would be widespread heartbreak over what happened, and communicated with his fans via his Twitter account. He wrote: 'just as disappointed as everyone else. I woke up this morning to the police cancelling the show for safety reasons. I love my fans . . . I love it here in Australia . . . and I want to sing."

Next up, he was travelling to New Zealand for a television appearance and to appear at a school that had won the visit in a competition. 'NEW ZEALAND we are coming!!!' announced Justin on Twitter. As that nation's girls began to get excited about what was ahead, Justin's team could only hope that this visit would pass off without any upset.

Justin reminded everyone that the safety of his fans was the top priority. 'I'm very happy about the welcome and the love from around the world, but I want everyone to still remember my fans' safety comes first . . .' Meanwhile, staff at Auckland Airport announced that special security measures would be put in place for Justin's arrival.

If Justin found it hard to believe the whirlwind of excitement he generated wherever he went then so did his mother. She was amazed at how pushy and excitable Justin's fans could get. Sometimes it was not just the fans who behaved this way, but their mothers too! 'The mothers are the worst,' said Pattie. During the melee at Auckland Airport Pattie was knocked over.

For Justin, who dearly loves his mother, this was enormously upsetting. During the wild madness Justin also had his hat stolen by one 'fan'. As the crush and pushing escalated, several fans began to hyperventilate. 'Oh My God! He was so amazing and beautiful. I can't believe I saw him,' one told reporters. Many of the fans had painted slogans such as 'I Love Bieber' on their faces. Meanwhile, the fan who had grabbed Justin's hat claimed that she would be sleeping with it.

He Tweeted his followers to express his disappointment at what happened. 'Finally got to New Zealand last night. The airport was crazy. Not happy that someone stole my hat and knocked down my mama. Come on people.' This is a hard line for Justin to tread.

He loves his fans and he's enormously proud of how devoted they are to him; he would never want to feel he was turning on his fans – but there was a line beyond which he would lose patience, particularly when his mother was involved. 'I want to be able to sign and take pics and meet my fans but if you are all pushing security won't let me,' he posted. 'Let's keep it safe and have fun.'

As for Pattie, she was shaken, but she Tweeted her own followers to assure them that she was OK after what happened. 'Thanks for all ur support!! I'm ok thank you!!!' she wrote.

Justin was later reunited with his hat, as he revealed on Twitter. 'I got my hat back. No hugs. no thanks u's. Just glad they did the right thing. I don't condone thievery!!'

Once he was through the airport chaos Justin fulfilled the engagements he had arranged for the New Zealand trip. He was asked on C4's *Select Live* show what his ideal girlfriend would be like. 'I'm looking for a girl who's funny, who can make me laugh, someone who's down to earth, with a nice smile [and] someone who can cook, because I can't cook,' he said.

When he moved on to the school – Strathallan High School in Auckland – he sat down to join a music lesson. 'What are we gonna play? Some Ozzy Osbourne or Led Zeppelin?' he asked. He was told that the song they would actually be learning was called 'Rain', a song by Kiwi rock act Dragon. 'Oh, I've never heard of that,' said Justin.

The fans who got to meet him had definitely heard of him and his music, though. They were transfixed by Justin. 'I was speechless when I first saw him,' said one fifteen-year-old later. 'I couldn't believe he was so beautiful, I just stared at him.'

While in New Zealand Justin also took part in a bungee jump – talk about living dangerously! 'I got to bungee jump this morning. The first time I went I was a little scared, so the second time I went backwards,' he reported. Wearing an all-black outfit and held safe by bright yellow harnesses, Justin looked more bumble bee than bungee, but he seemed to love the adrenalin of the moment.

Another event had to be cancelled when Justin travelled in Europe. An appearance in Paris had to be cut short when too many fans arrived to see him. 'Sorry to any of the kids I didn't get to meet,' he Tweeted afterwards. 'I love all of you for your support.' In the wake of the chaos in New Zealand and other areas, Justin was asked if the obsession his fans had for him had got out of hand. He told a CNN television interviewer that he did not agree that his fans are 'too obsessed'. Added Justin: 'Nah, you know, I think my fans are really supportive and I'm glad that I have really devoted fans. You know, I guess they do what they gotta do.'

All the same, he has admitted that he feels overwhelmed and a bit scared sometimes. 'When I was in Seattle, this girl came out of nowhere and she tried to hug me, but she tackled me instead,' he told *Seventeen* magazine. 'It was really scary.'

He has also stated that he remains grateful for the opportunities his fame has created for him. 'It's been pretty amazing and I'm really glad that I've just been able to do what I love,' he said. 'I'm really glad that I get to travel the world and like I said, just do what I love to do.' He could afford to be happy and proud, for he had another engagement with the President of the United States of America just round the corner.

8

Sweet Sixteen

The early months of 2010 had seen Justin become one of the most discussed celebrities on the planet. It was not just his fan base who knew all about him. People everywhere were becoming aware of the kid from Canada who had launched a phenomenal music career from YouTube. He had already had a string of hit records, appeared on top television programmes and sparked scenes of fan mayhem that reminded many older observers of the 'Beatlemania' that greeted British rock band The Beatles wherever they travelled in the 1960s.

All this was remarkable enough, but the fact that he only turned sixteen in March made it little short of astonishing. If Justin had already enjoyed such success before his sixteenth birthday, what might lie ahead for him in the future? Would he be a 'flash in the pan' pop star who would be as quickly forgotten by the fans as they had adopted him?

As he celebrated his birthday, all the indications were that the former scenario would come true and that Justin would go on to build a hugely successful and lasting career. His party was a fun night, with his mentor Usher among the guests. There was basketball, paintball, sumo wrestling and laser tag games among the fun. Usher bought Justin quite a present. 'He bought me a Range Rover,' Justin revealed on *Live On Studio Five.* 'I can drive.'

In another interview he revealed that before he became famous one of Justin's biggest career hopes was to become a man who fixes cars. 'I always wanted to be a car mechanic,' he told Jay Leno. Instead, he became a pop star.

In the same month that he turned sixteen, Justin released the second part of his debut album. *My World 2.0* hit the stores in the middle of the month. Starting with the joyful 'Baby' and also including the uptempo 'Somebody to Love' and the smooch-worthy 'U Smile', it is a wonderful piece of work. 'I wanna thank you guys for everything,' he said on his YouTube video marking the release. Again, there was a golden ticket competition tied to the album's release. 'Make sure to go get the album,' he said, 'and thanks very much.'

An MTV show called *The Diary of Justin Bieber* helped raise his profile even further in March. It gave an interesting behind-the-scenes glimpse into Justin's glamorous but sometimes wild world. 'Be careful,' he said on the show, 'cos it can get crazy out there.'

The cameras followed him to the French capital of Paris, where his tour man Kenny was shown persuading Justin to get up and out of bed so they could get to work. Viewers then see Justin getting his famous hairstyle ready in the hotel bathroom. Then his on-the-road tutor Jenny gives Justin a class. With the mixture of japes, work and sightseeing of Justin's trip, the show becomes an entertaining look into his world as he promotes *My World 2.0*. He is even shown exchanging tense words with Pattie as they are driven to a performance. 'She has to understand I'm fifteen,' he explains later in a piece-to-camera. It was an entertaining and sweet show for viewers. For Justin it was a great way to promote his new releases.

The next two singles to be released from *My World 2.0* were 'U Smile' and 'Somebody to Love'. Bieber helped write 'U Smile', a sweet mid-tempo tune that again encourages the listener to feel they are at one with Justin and very much a part of his world.

'I wrote it for all my fans who got me here,' Justin said about the song. The About.com website was impressed, saying that 'U Smile' 'is guaranteed to generate warm and fuzzy emotions in millions of young fans'. Meanwhile, *Billboard* believed that the song would have a wider appeal than that, arguing that it 'should appeal to some older listeners'. It reached Number 17 in the Canadian chart.

'Somebody to Love' was released in June. The song had originally been recorded in demo form by Usher, before being passed for proper recording and release by Justin. Usher sang backing vocals on Justin's recording. The BBC Music webpage was impressed, describing the song as, 'a straightforward plea for a soul mate; it says something we've all felt'. The accompanying video showed Justin dancing alongside top quality dancers. At the end of the filming, in which Justin dancing alongside Usher, he said of his mentor, 'He tried to show me up but I showed him up!'

On Easter Sunday he performed for the President again at the Easter Egg roll at the White House. This annual event is held on the White House lawn for children and their parents. Wearing a maroon T-shirt and tight black jeans, Justin took to the stage with more confidence than seen at his previous Presidential engagement. For the 2010 event President Obama had chosen a theme of 'Ready, Set, Go!' for the Easter Egg roll, to promote 'health and wellness'.

The President's wife introduced Justin, saying, 'You can go over to the music stage and just have some fun with Justin Bieber. You guys know Justin Bieber? You've heard of Justin Bieber? Well, he's here.' Justin showed himself to be in great health on the day. He filled the performance on the South Lawn of the White House with exciting songs, including his hit 'One Time'. 'What a lovely crowd,' he said during his set. 'They're hyped a little bit!' agreed one of his band. 'How many of you guys think it's a beautiful day out here? It's a beautiful day! I see everyone's smiling out there. It's a good time to play my new song, "U Smile".'

There was yet more fun to come. He sang the iconic rap song 'Walk This Way', which was such a hit for the New York hip-hop act Run-DMC in the 1980s. He also performed a hearty drum solo. He then jumped onto the main part of the stage and asked the audience 'You ready?' The audience cheered as Justin performed his hit single 'Baby'.

'Thank you very much everybody,' he said as the song came to a spectacular conclusion. What a day it had been for the audience. Among the other performers featured were the cast of the hit television series *Glee*. Indeed, it was Amber Riley who had alone opened the festivities with a performance of 'The Star-Spangled Banner'.

Justin played it cool when he looked back on the day. 'Basically, we went to Washington. We did the thing for the president,' he said casually to *MTV News*. 'It was great,' he added. '[Obama] was really cool, really nice, and I was just happy to be there. We met them, took pictures with them, took pictures with the first lady.'

On Twitter he later wrote again about his latest encounter with the President. 'The first time I met him was a couple months back,' Bieber said. 'And when he introduced me, he said, "Justin Bye-ber". 'I got to hang out with him in the Oval Office, which is pretty crazy, because no one really gets to go in there,' he said. 'But it was pretty incredible. I got pictures with him.' He continued: 'I got to go into the White House and get a tour and a pic with the first family. They are really nice and had a lot of fun. But after three performances in 90 degree hot sun I'm completely dehydrated and almost passed out after the last one . . . need to drink some water,' he continued. 'Thanks to everyone who came out today . . . it was a pretty incredible experience and I am grateful for the honor. Thanks to all the fans.'

April was a wonderful month for Justin. So many exciting things were happening for him that he could scarcely keep up with it all himself! The month also saw him make chart history when he became the youngest solo male artist to have a Number 1 on the *Billboard* Top 200 since Stevie Wonder. Justin's *My World 2.0* took the top position, while his debut *My World* remained in the Top 5, making him the youngest male ever to achieve this. 'Wake up to some incredible news … how do we celebrate?' wrote Justin on Twitter. 'WE DID IT!!! I OWE ALL OF U!! THANK U,' he added.

Another exciting moment for Justin came when he appeared on the legendary American entertainment television show *Saturday Night Live*. He sang 'Baby' and 'U Smile', as well as performing a short comedy routine alongside host Tina Fey. 'Will never forget 2nite. It was INCREDIBLE!!' he wrote afterwards on Twitter. 'Thank u for the opportunity and thanks to everyone at *SNL* and Tina Fey for just being fun.' The Showbiz Spy website claimed that 'insiders' at the show were of the opinion that Justin had a crush on Fey. 'Justin has a serious case of puppy love. He followed her around backstage like a pet Labrador,' said the sources.

With this increasing success making him not just a star but a superstar, Justin had to face the downside of huge fame – increased attention and scrutiny from the media. For instance, a joke that Justin had made about a member of his team was to come back and haunt them both. 'I have a swagger coach that helps me and teaches me different swaggerific things to do,' he had said. Justin was referring to a man called Ryan Good, whose official job title is 'road manager'. Good, previously an assistant to Usher, described Justin as 'A talented dude, with a personality the size of the world.' He explained how he came to work with Justin, saying: 'Usher thought I would be a good influence on him – kind of cool, you know, positive.' Good added that having people to guide a pop star is by no means unheard of. 'Lots of artists go through "refinement boot camp",' he explained. 'Justin's a sponge, a bright kid. But he's still just fifteen.'

As the media began to routinely describe Good as the 'swagger coach' both he and Justin felt embarrassed at the description. Later in the year there were to be even more uncomfortable headlines for Justin when rumours were spread that he misbehaved at the Radio 1 Big Weekend in the UK and then swore at staff on a TV show in Australia.

Justin was upset by these stories, which he felt were inaccurate. He was able to use his Twitter feed to get his side of the story direct to his fans. 'Family time with my mum couldn't come at a better time,' he wrote in the aftermath of these stories. 'i was raised to respect others and not gossip . . . nor answer gossip with anger. I know my friends, family and fans know the person i am. hearing adults spread lies and rumours is part of the job i guess. So everyone keep smiling . . . we r all blessed and I am still grateful and appreciate of the opportunity u have all given me to do what i love.'

Having worked so hard and being so successful in building up such a huge Twitter following – over 3 million strong at the time of writing – Justin deserves to have such a powerful and instant way to put his side of the story across. In another example, he has twice been rumoured to have died and was able to confirm this was not true via Twitter. In truth, he is likely to face unpleasant stories and rumours at times in the future. All celebrities do, but at least he can rest assured that he can respond quickly.

His popularity on Twitter meant that for many months his name was always in the top of the 'Trending Topics' section, meaning that 'Justin Bieber' was one of the most typed phrases on the website. In May 2010 the website owners changed the programming of the site so that priority was given to words and phrases that enjoy sudden popularity, at the expense of terms – like Justin Bieber – that are more regularly Tweeted in large volume. This meant that his name disappeared from the Trending Topics, but the mere fact that Twitter felt the need to make such a move is a tribute to what a phenomenal success Justin has become.

Still, Justin's fans were not about to become outfoxed by Twitter that easily. They began to Tweet about 'Bustin Jieber' – Justin's name with the first letter of each word swapped – and that was quickly trending. You cannot keep the Justin Bieber fan base down for long and Justin was both touched and amused by their gesture.

In May his prestige was also confirmed on television when he was invited to appear on the legendary *Oprah* show. 'Today's show is for anyone who has sung into the mirror, pretended that their hairbrush was a microphone and imagined singing on stage to millions,' said Oprah Winfrey in her introduction. Justin touched the hands of girls in the audience as he walked on to join Oprah on the set. When he reached the famous host they hugged fondly. The girls in the audience continued to scream and cry, to Oprah's disbelief. 'All right,' she said to the girls. 'Can we talk?'

They spoke about Justin's rise to fame and how he felt about life in the spotlight. Pattie and Scooter Braun were also on the set and Pattie spoke about how she felt about her son. He confirmed that his mother helped keep his feet on the ground and would confiscate his mobile phone if he misbehaved. He also sang his hit 'Baby', much to the screaming delight of the girls in the studio audience.

Capping off a wonderful appearance, he finished the song on the drum kit with a mind-blowing drum solo. He grinned sweetly and swapped salutes with Oprah. Television appearances did not get much bigger than this and he remained confident throughout. 'It felt great,' he said backstage once his slot was finished.

In the summer of 2009, as he prepared for his first ever world tour, Justin's popularity showed no sign of declining. Indeed, the frenzy around him was actually intensifying. When he was photographed alongside glamorous socialite Kim Kardashian on the beach in the Bahamas, Justin was reminded just how intense his fans' feelings for him can be. 'Look, it's my girlfriend,' Justin wrote on Twitter in reference to the photographs.

It was only meant as a joke, but some fans failed to see the funny side of his quip. Many bombarded Kardashian with hateful messages on Twitter. Some of these nasty messages were said to include threats on her life. 'I was getting the craziest messages from all of the Beliebers,' she told *Us* magazine. She asked Justin if he could stop the fans from abusing and threatening her. 'ladies calm down,' Justin pleaded on his Twitter page. '@kimkardashian is a friend. a very sexy friend but a friend. no need 4 threats.'

As Justin adjusts to the level of intensity his fans feel towards him he is also learning how to react responsibly to crazy situations. Whether it means he has to cancel an appearance for the safety of his fans, or lightly admonish the fans who knocked over his mother at an airport or sent death threats to Kardashian, Justin will always try to react the right way. After all, he knows that the vast majority of his fans are kind girls who would never do anything to upset him or anyone else.

As Justin heads into the future, he lives a strange but fun existence. He has to work hard and make many sacrifices, but in return he receives adulation, fame and increasing fortune. Quite simply, over the past two years Justin has not lived the life of a normal teenage boy.

Neither is his life likely to become anywhere approaching normal in the foreseeable future. Those who surround Justin as he works are all much older than him, which has given him an interesting perspective on growing up. 'I am with adults all day,' said Bieber of his current team, 'and it's fun sometimes, but sometimes I'd rather hang out with my friends my own age. But at the same time, it makes me mature a little faster. I think I'm still immature sometimes, but I try not to think I'm hot stuff.' However, much as some rumour-mongers have tried to portray him as arrogant or badly-behaved, all the real evidence points to Justin as a sweet and generous boy.

There can be no denying that he is fanatically popular. Many around the world have watched with huge surprise as his popularity soars and soars. They are right to be surprised, Justin is as shocked as everyone else. 'I don't really understand it, because I've never had a musician I was that into,' he said of his fans' devotion to him. 'I just try to make it as fun for them as possible. For some of them, this might be the only time they'll get to meet me.' In this sense Justin is unlike many other famous young people.

Take, for instance, famous young sports stars. In most cases they will have grown up idolizing other famous sports stars themselves, so as they in turn become idolized for their skills, they know what it feels like to idolize another skilful player of their particular sport. Justin, however, has had to adjust to being the focus of these feelings without the same reference point from his own past.

The way he has adjusted so well to fame has pleasantly surprised those around him. 'It's like Justin has already been here before,' said Usher. 'Although he's sixteen, when you talk to him, it's like you're talking to a well-seasoned young man. It's almost like he'd already mapped out in his mind what his story could be, and it's up to us to navigate him.' That 'navigation' means that – in some ways – Justin has grown up faster than other kids.

However, he can still be a very cheeky boy. Backstage at a television show Justin was due to perform at he was believed to have had a bit of fun by hiding his tutor Jenny's mobile phone. 'Justin, did you take my phone?' she said, realizing it had vanished. 'Because if you don't have it, I'm going to have to cancel my plan right now.' Justin was innocence itself, and replied: 'No! I swear, I didn't take it,' he said. Jenny was not entirely convinced. 'I don't know. It's April Fools' Day,' she sighed, 'and he's a sixteen-year-old boy.' Her phone was later returned to her – though she never discovered for sure who the culprit was.

One April Fools' prank that Justin was involved in came on the comedy website Funny Or Die. 'Anything that's not Bieber dies,' he said on the prank video. 'I'm a star. I do what stars do. I ride on yachts. I autograph lady lumps. And I pay people to slap them. Sometimes I don't feel like walking so I make enormous people carry me around. I talk loudly in libraries and I swim directly after I eat. I don't care.' He continued: 'So remember, this is Bieber's world. You're just living in it. Bieber or die.'

He has always had a real sense of humour and Justin is simply too full of life and fun to keep down for long. Even on the rare moments that Justin does need an encouraging chat, he is surrounded by people who are more than willing and equipped to give it to him. His mother is always there and sometimes his father accompanies him on the road as well. Even those team members who are not related to Justin by blood feel like they are family sometimes. 'Sometimes he's like a little brother or a son to me,' said Usher.

With all this love surrounding him Justin can hardly go far wrong. But what of his prospects of getting a different kind of love, by finding a girl to share his life with?

Justin has spoken about the sort of girl that he would like to date. He told *People* magazine that he was looking for a date with 'nice eyes and a nice smile, a girl that can make me laugh, because everybody likes to laugh'. He then added that he had not been on a date for three years, and admitted he was keen to change this as: 'I just really love girls!'

It is not all about looks for Justin. Personality is very important to him when it comes to girls. 'You can have the hottest girl in the world but if at the end of the day you can't sit there and have a conversation with her it's going to be terrible,' he told a backstage interviewer after his *Oprah* appearance.

Justin is honest about his life and admits he once treated a girl in a way he now regrets. 'I have dumped a girl over the phone – it's terrible isn't it?' he told *Top of the Pops* magazine. 'We got into an argument during a phone call so I basically said, "I don't wanna be with you any more."

She cried. I saw her after that and it was a bit awkward, but we're not enemies now, so that's cool. But I wouldn't recommend it, it's very mean!'

Justin has learned lessons already in his young life, but the question is still often asked of him: how can he sing so much about love before he is even out of his teens? 'I think at any age you can experience love,' he insists. 'Whether you're eighty or five, you're always gonna ... I don't know. There's a difference between love and being in love because you can love someone but not necessarily be in love. So I think I've loved girls, but I don't know – I haven't been *in* love before.'

He will now have to live out any future romances in the public eye. Indeed, all the changes he goes through as he matures will happen in the glare of the flashbulb. As Justin grows older his voice is changing and developing, and he will have to adapt his music to fit – he has already had to change the key he sings 'Baby' in as he is now unable to reach the highest notes in the original key. 'It cracks,' he said of his voice. 'Like every teenage boy, I'm dealing with it and I have the best vocal coach in the world.'

He also has dreams of future collaborations, including with soul singer Beyoncé and hip-hop star Kanye West. As he works on his new album – which he is set to record in New York – Justin will have lots of fresh ideas for new musical directions. He has been working with, among others, a British soul singer called Taio Cruz. Ambitious, dedicated and energetic, Justin will not stand still. Whatever changes he makes to his sound and image, the one thing that will hopefully remain is Justin's unique charm, which comes from being the small-town boy with the sweet smile and even sweeter voice who made it big thanks to his home-made YouTube videos.

So here's to a bright future for Justin Bieber. As the young man himself said when assessing the massive success he has enjoyed: 'Every so often, I think, "Wow." But I don't know. I just don't think about it. I just take it one day at a time.'

Index

Picture Credits

Select Websites

Bibliography

Justin Bieber: The Unauthorised Biography, by Ronny Bloom, Sunbird 2010
100% Justin Bieber: The Unofficial Biography, by Evie Parker, Bantam 2010
The Justin Bieber Annual 2011, by Tori Kosara, Buster Books 2010